"With a deft touch and lively spirit, Eric Clayton has written nothing less than a vibrant screenplay for the spiritual life. This book addresses the imagination, stirs the heart, and invites one to undertake a pilgrimage that has the potential to change one's life. Clayton proves himself a worthy apprentice to Obi-Wan Kenobi: With this book, he empowers readers to take their 'first steps into a larger world' where they may encounter Christ in the most unexpected places."

—Fr. Ryan Duns, SJ, professor and author of *Theology of Horror: The Hidden Depths of Popular Films*

~

"If you want to "get" speculative storytelling—fantasy, science fiction, and the like—you have to dwell with it. You have to inhabit the world being presented to you. You have to let it wash over you, so that you see the world through the eyes of your favorite author or moviemaker or storyteller. The same, it turns out, goes for the spiritual life, and for the kind of attitude we must cultivate if we are to perceive in creation the imaginative hand of its Author. Eric Clayton has dwelt with both speculative storytelling and the spiritual life. In *Where Wonder Leads*, he shows us how the imagination we cultivate through storytelling can enrich our spiritual lives. And then, just as any good storyteller or spiritual guide does, he invites us into the adventure."

—Joseph M. Vukov, PhD, Associate Director, The Hank Center for the Catholic Intellectual Heritage

~

"Clayton's book is a loving invitation to remember that the movements of the Holy Spirit are always more dynamic and inviting than we can imagine—and indeed it may be through the extraordinary God-given gift of our imaginations that we are best able to feel them transform us."

—Susan Haarman, PhD, Director of Campus Partnerships, Interfaith America, and author of *Roll for Discernment: Dungeon Master as St. Ignatius' Spiritual Director.*

~

"As kids, we all knew, deep down, that we were destined to be heroes. We fought dragons, saw magic in every corner of God's world, and wondered, "Does Dad believe in fairies, too?" Eric Clayton's *Where Wonder Leads* guides the reader back to those heroic moments of childhood through the imagination, exploring the richness of fairyland, to enrich our souls once more."

—Rose John Sheffler, author, *Past Watchful Dragons: Biblical Stories Retold*

~

"The constant yearning of our soul is to find deep and purposeful spiritual meaning to our life. Eric Clayton tells us how, shows us how, and then leads us on the way. This book is the map, the sign, the path, and the guide. But this book is no simple step-by-step, just add water, guide of exercises of the Ignatian Way. Clayton is a poet, and this book is an adventure into the hinterland of Faerie. But Clayton is also a prophet, who uses Ignatius to call us to ourselves and to God, demonstrating how to take the imagination of The Good, make it tangible, and begin to change not only our world, but the entire world. This is the book I have needed to read—and wished I could have written."

—Sonya Shetty Cronin, PhD, Florida State University Department of Religion & International Programs, Executive Director of The Carrier Pigeon Post

Where Wonder Leads

Other Books by Eric A. Clayton

Finding Peace Here and Now: How Ignatian Spirituality Leads Us to Healing and Wholeness

My Life with the Jedi: The Spirituality of Star Wars

Cannonball Moments: Telling Your Story, Deepening Your Faith

The Seagull on the Chapel: A Story of Value and Worth

Our Mother Too: Mary Embraces the World

ERIC A. CLAYTON

WHERE WONDER LEADS

FINDING GOD *Through* FAIRY TALES, MYTH, *and* CONTEMPLATIVE PRAYER

LOYOLA PRESS.
A JESUIT MINISTRY

LOYOLA PRESS.
A JESUIT MINISTRY
www.loyolapress.com

Cover art: user135743/iStock/Getty Images, Pablo Ramon de Lima Pinheiro/iStock/Getty Image
Interior art: user135743/iStock/Getty Images, aleksandarvelasevic/DigitalVision Vectors/Getty Images, Alhontess/iStock/Getty Images, Pablo Ramon de Lima Pinheiro/iStock/Getty Images, oixxo/iStock/Getty Images
Author photo: Allison Clayton

ISBN: 978-0-8294-6065-0
Library of Congress Control Number: 2026940152

Published in Chicago, IL
Printed in Canada
26 27 28 29 30 31 32 33 34 35 MQS 10 9 8 7 6 5 4 3 2 1

For anyone who has ever wondered

if wondering is a worthy prayer.

May this book be an affirmation.

Contents

PART III TOOLS FOR SHARING

Introduction

This book is a call to adventure. It's also an invitation to a profound experience of prayer. What you hold in your hands was written to nourish, sustain, and affirm your imagination as a pathway to that which is holy, sacred, and mystical. But in these spiritual hinterlands, it's always wise to have a guide to accompany you along the way. And so, think of this book as a travel companion through the fantastical realms of myth and wonder.

Through thirty-five guided meditations rooted in the Catholic (and, in particular, the Ignatian) tradition, this book will challenge you to step into a larger world, to imagine yourself assuming the role of the epic hero, and to reflect upon what such responsibility demands of you, as well as what it reveals about your truest self. Why guided meditations? Because through them, you exercise that crucial tool of prayer and reflection: the imagination. Through our imagination, we enter into dialogue with our God who has great dreams for us, dreams we may not yet fully see but that unfold, often and at first in hidden places, in our lives. How can we begin to envision what we do not completely understand? Only through the imagination. This is where we encounter the living God.

This book is for anyone who has ever found more spiritual truth in fairy tales than in a sermon; for those who pray better with stories than with syllabi; for those who make pilgrimages to the Renaissance Faire just as frequently as to shrines and grottos; for seekers and skeptics who suspect that our imaginations were always meant to point us back to God. This book was written so that you might rediscover enchantment in your prayer life by engaging with the symbols, creatures, and themes of fantasy literature, pop culture, movies, fairy tales, myth, and more. Whether it's a wizard on your doorstep or a walking stick left behind, these tropes and archetypes hold spiritual insights. This book will help you pray, reflect, and imagine your way toward a deeper encounter with grace in a unique way, one that engages your imagination along the essential path you've been invited to embark on.

In part I, I provide three essays to set the stage for our adventure.

In part II, you'll find the contemplative guided meditations—go ahead and jump to page 33 if you want to get started! These contemplations can be read at your own pace, either in a retreat setting or prayed daily. Each presents a stereotypical fantasy motif. Perhaps you're the one who is greeted by the wizard, or perhaps you're the one who is tempted to slay a captured orc. How do you respond?

Every contemplation is broken into three parts:

- **Step into adventure** invites you to imagine yourself in the story, engaging with fantasy motifs as though you were a character in the tale. What do you see and feel in these moments? How does this fantastical encounter resonate with your innermost self?
- **Turn to the ordinary** provides a brief essay in which I share reflections and lessons that relate the spiritual themes of each contemplation to my own life. This is an opportunity for you to consider how these mythic motifs are unfolding in *your* daily life.

- **Cross the threshold** is an opportunity to harmonize the first and second parts. Return to the second-person guided meditation newly informed by how your ordinary daily life is illuminated by these fantastical themes. How does a return to the story invite you to carry these mythic motifs into your life and community?

There is more than one way to navigate these pages. This book can be read straight through as you might read a fantasy novel. It can be prayed with daily as part of your reflective practice. It can be grappled with communally on retreat. (Check out the appendices in part III for ideas and activities to use in the classroom, on retreat, with your family, and more!) But regardless of your approach, remember that this is an adventure into prayer—a journey that you can make again and again. Each time you embark on this road, you are necessarily different. Your own context changes; your own experiences continue to unfold. And so, begin by reflecting on who you are today, now, at this very moment. Who *is* this character (you!) that is about to set off on a thrilling quest? What is this character (you!) hoping to find? And how will this character (you!) be changed by the road ahead?

Let's begin.

Pray-er Worksheet: Reflecting on Character

I am ____,

and my adventure begins on ___________________________.

What is the grace you seek from this adventure? Humility? Understanding of purpose? Strength to make a big decision?

____

____

____

____

What are your strengths?

____

____

____

What opportunities for growth stretch out before you?

Is there a holy or wise person, living or deceased, you turn to for guidance in your life? What actions can you take from their insights?

What spiritual tools do you carry on this journey? Your rosary? Prayer cards? Icons? Miraculous medals?

What was your previous spiritual journey? Was it made during a pilgrimage? A retreat? Reading a book that really spoke to you?

What insights did you acquire on that journey that can be brought along on this adventure?

What words of power might you invoke as you set off? Write your prayer to guide you through your journey.

PART I

The Framing

As we set out upon our chosen path, we are guided by a simple yet all-encompassing question: Why? There are countless ways to encounter God; why should we spend time chasing the Sacred by way of the Fantastical? And why do so using tools and traditions of Catholic spirituality? Most important, why do we feel this call? In these opening three chapters, I invite you to sink into these questions, and allow the essays that follow to frame your own thinking. The frame is important: It dictates what we ultimately are able to see. And so, as we take our first steps into the world of Fairie, be mindful of your why—and of the questions that can expand your reframed vision.

CHAPTER ONE

A Catholic Imagination in Speculative Storytelling

The fairy garden is in disarray.

Wind and rain have battered the tiny painted structures. The fairy houses stand nestled on a rock in the shadow of a tall crepe myrtle from which a flurry of pink petals has fallen. They're dead now—brown, decaying, clumpy. The little structures themselves are faded: Bright reds have become pale pinks; highlight yellows have turned nearly white. The inhabitants of this small landscape-bound community are in no better shape. The gnomes have been toppled; the fairies are on their sides. Even the dragon, tasked with protecting the small village, has succumbed to the wind. The great pink creature faces a completely arbitrary direction, offering hardly any protection.

"Will you help me fix it?" My eldest daughter stands with her hands on her hips, curls tumbling about her shoulders. "We can't leave the fairy garden like that."

I purse my lips, rub the back of my neck. I have other things to do. These are her toys after all.

"You can do it," I say.

"I can't," she insists. "I need your help. The fairies will never come if the fairy garden looks like that."

She's got a point. "Fine. Show me what you need."

For the next twenty minutes, I squat alongside Elianna, carefully taking each of the fairy garden pieces in one hand and rinsing them off with the hose I hold in the other. There are too many spider webs, Elianna insists. We need to get rid of those. Camira—my youngest—concurs.

"Aren't spiders good for a fairy garden?" I ask. "Same size and all, right?"

I'm a fool. Spiders are not good for a fairy garden. No speck of web nor wayward piece of dirt will be tolerated. I suppose the fairies could get stuck in the web, eaten by the spider. Perhaps I'm not thinking this all the way through.

I wash off each individual piece—the little people, the little homes, the little chairs and table—and then turn my hose on the rock.

"You missed some bird poop," Elianna says, pointing. I say she can hose the rock off herself if she's going to be so picky.

"I think we need a second rock," she says instead, once the first is clear and clean. "The fairies need more room."

I can't say I disagree. I haul another flat piece of stone over and lay it next to the first, still nestled in the shadow of the crepe myrtle. "We can use this bridge to connect the two," I say, proffering one of the now-clean fairy garden pieces. Elianna nods. Like that was the most obvious statement in the world. We proceed to rebuild the fairy garden, placing each denizen of the village and miniature structure in its proper location.

When the work is done, we stand back and admire this piece of fairyland that sits snugly in our front yard.

"The fairies are going to like this," Elianna says with a grin. I nod, smile back. I believe they will. And I still have time to mow the lawn. But I'm glad that I've taken the time to rebuild this little fairy-tale village. And why?

This was more than a half-decent attempt at parenting. I've replied to my kids' requests for crafts and games with a confident "No" on plenty of occasions. After all, how else would the lawn ever get mowed?

But this was different. The fairy garden isn't just a game, though it is that and more. It isn't just an outdoor craft, though art and color abound. Sitting with my daughters in the mud and the mulch, propping up fading fairy-tale creatures was something else entirely. This was an affirmation of imagination, the participation in its upkeep and refueling. This was a near-mystical experience, a huddling together at a gateway that opens not simply into our front yard but also into the land of Faerie, a land of elves and wizards, of talking trees and wise wolves. This was a father and his children daring to partake in something beyond our knowing, beyond the seen and the understood, something that points to a world that transcends the one we inhabit, a world of myth and magic and unbound possibility.

This was a near religious experience. As a Catholic who is deeply formed by a Catholic imagination—which, in the words of Fr. Andrew Greeley, "sees created reality as a 'sacrament,' that is, a revelation of the presence of God"—I am always ready and eager to see in the ordinary materials of our days something *more*, something *other*, something *mystical*.[1]

We did not bless ourselves or recite well-worn prayers. We held no rosary beads and found no holy water. And yet, we still oriented our minds and hearts in the direction of mystery. In the humble offering of hand-painted figurines and dying flower petals, we once more affirmed that creation is vast and beyond our wildest imaginings, that it is dripping with the sacred. In the humdrum preparation of a fairy garden and the hope-filled wondering that such magical creatures might pay our home a visit, we dared imagine that which we've never truly seen. We prepared a space for those unknown visitors, and in so doing, tilled the soil of our imagination to look for and expect not fairies but God's own self.

This is the foundation of a sacramental imagination, one that sees the ordinary raw material of our days as graced, as pulsing with potential, as pointing beyond the known and piercing the veil into the sacred. I desperately want this for my daughters. I want it for myself, too. I want to nourish it, share it, watch it grow and flourish. For me, this sort of imagination is fed in the lands of Middle-earth, Westeros, and Narnia, around a game table cluttered with cards and dice and handwritten notes, through the wielding of swords with names and the casting of spells meant to elevate the good and the beautiful.

This sort of imagination makes room for a God that is far greater than we know, far beyond what our human minds can conjure, and yet intimately present in our mundane, nitty-gritty lives. This sort of imagination seeks after this wild and mysterious God, looking for clues, for breadcrumbs, for hidden thresholds across which God's Spirit calls, invites, whispers. This sort of imagination is humbly offered to the Creator, who wishes to use the raw material of our curiosities, wonderings, and awe to make manifest something fantastical.

A Jesuit, a Psychologist, and a Professor Walk into a Fairy Tale

Have you ever wondered why these worlds of legend and lore call to you? Why at times they feel more real and relevant than even the most respected literary novels? Why they resonate with your own spiritual seeking in ways that you can't quite put a finger on? I have.

These questions have burned in my heart since I was a child. Now, I watch those same flames flicker to life in my own children. Where did these questions come from?

I know where my girls have learned about fairy-tale creatures. We've watched plenty of Disney movies together. We've read fantastical stories before bedtime. And I've observed the games they play with their friends. I am well familiar with the source material that has planted the seed of myth and magic in their little heads.

But what about that very first person for whom the notion of a fairy was radical and novel and unheard of? Think for a moment on those early pioneers to the land of Faerie: the ones who didn't have access to the Disney vault of fairy-tale films; who came long before a hobbit trekked into unknown lands with a pesky piece of jewelry; who were born even before those gods of Nordic, Roman, and Greek mythology, before Thor and Zeus and Mars. Ponder the dreamers whose imaginations first thought, *Might there be strange and mysterious Others among us, here yet beyond our vision, hidden yet real and present?*

Carl Jung, the Swiss psychologist who revolutionized how we think about the human psyche, had a lot to say about myth and its place in our minds and culture. To start, Jung claims that humans could not have invented the ideas of gods and mythic creatures. Rather, these ideas are bound up in who we are, in how we are made. These stories we tell and parallels we draw by observing the natural world are simply the manifestation of what we already have buried within us. We don't dream up a sun god by observing the sun; something within us already knows the Divine, and the sun simply calls to mind that truth. "Humans can only project onto the world gods already in their minds," mythology scholar Robert A. Segal writes of Jung's thinking.[2] "Jung contends that everyone is born not merely with a need of some kind that the invention of myth fulfills but with myths themselves."[3] For Jung, we are all born with the raw material of myth in our very DNA: "Myths are original revelations of the preconscious psyche, involuntary statements about unconscious psychic happenings."[4] And he claims that this impulse is present in the collective unconscious of everyone.

For us people of faith, it makes sense to believe that God wove these stories within us. God continues to speak to us still through these stories, through the mythic structure alive within each person. Is that why the Christ story resonates so strongly? Not because we've made Jesus into a mythic hero but because the rhythm of myth is the natural way in which God desires to speak to us. And Jesus, in leaving his heavenly home, stepping into the proverbial unknown, descending into darkness, and rising once more with new wisdom to share with others, fulfills that story.

The myths and the fantastical stories they tell us—the stories *we* tell through *them*—are already living within us. "Myths for moderns do not function to connect the inner world with the outer world, which remains impersonal and mechanical," Segal writes. "Instead, modern myths function to connect—better, to reconnect—moderns to the inner world."[5] The power of myth, then, is to reconnect us to the great Mythmaker, the one who has planted myth within each of us and yearns to see it lived out.

French Jesuit Pierre Teilhard de Chardin wrote, "The deeper I descend into myself, the more I find God at the heart of my being; the more I multiply the links that attach me to things, the more closely does he hold me—the God who pursues in me the task, as endless as the whole sum of centuries, of the incarnation of his Son."[6] God has placed myth and fantasy within us already; as we pull on these threads of story, we come to know God more deeply and discover what God desires of us in our very real lives. As we plumb the depths of the story within us, we quite literally come to better understand our God and our part in God's story.

In his delightful graphic novel, *The Mythmakers: The Remarkable Fellowship of C.S. Lewis & J.R.R. Tolkien*, John Hendrix drops us into the moment when Professor Tolkien illuminates for Lewis the importance of myth to understanding the Christian life: "Christ is the myth that entered history," Tolkien proclaims. "He is the myth that actually came true. All the ancient myths are the refraction and splintering of God's true white light into the many colors we see throughout the world. We write myths because our hearts were written by a mythmaker."[7] We are made in the image and likeness of this Great Mythmaker. We write myths because there is more story to be told.

Jung sees in Jesus Christ a full realization of the heroic archetype: "But the ordinary man, too, unconsciously lives the archetypal forms." He continues, "What happens in the life of Christ happens always and everywhere."[8] Jesus tells us he is the way; we know we are called to follow him. Each of us is Christ present in the world. But have we ever truly considered that deep within our own stories is the story of Christ being written anew? That God speaks into our world through this same, all-encompassing mythic story?

Still, it can be tempting to dismiss fantasy, fairy tales, and myth. These stories don't deal with *real* life, right? They're focused on the magical, the fantastical, and the epic, never on the humdrum and the ordinary. But if what we've been reflecting on thus far is true, these stories may actually touch *more* deeply upon real life than other tales. "Fairy-stories deal largely, or (the better ones) mainly, with simple or fundamental things," Tolkien writes. But it's precisely because our ordinary world is, as Tolkien sees it, "untouched by Fantasy" that the casting of our *real* lives into imaginary lands makes them "all the more luminous by their setting."[9]

By entering the realm of Faerie, we see and understand our present lives with a nuance found nowhere else. Do the exaggerated stereotypes so often encountered in speculative storytelling help us better wrestle with and make sense of the myriad parts of our own inner lives? Consider *Star Trek*. Vulcans are simply human beings taken to an extreme—what if we allowed ourselves to be fully governed by logic with no credence given to emotion? Klingons are similar—what if our entire culture was centered on violence as a virtue? At first glance, these aliens seem foreign, but upon deeper reflection, we realize they are like funhouse mirrors held up to reflect certain aspects of our very selves. What do they reveal? There are other parts, too, for us to consider: the part of the hero, the part of the wizard, the part of the dragon, the part of the bard. Hold these archetypical characters up and see what they reveal within you.

But there's more reason to linger in Faerie. Tolkien insists that fairy-stories are marked by what he calls a *eucatastrophe*, or the very opposite of a catastrophe. It's "the joy of the happy ending: or more correctly of the good catastrophe, the sudden joyous 'turn.'" This word, "turn," is important to Tolkien because, like in real life, a good fairy-story has no conclusion. The story continues to unfold. It's not the end we're talking about but a new moment of significance. So, this idea of turning toward the sudden goodness of life, the surprising intervention of mystery and wonder, is essential. "In its fairy-tale—or otherworld—setting, it is a sudden and miraculous grace: never to be counted on to recur." Tolkien goes on to say that this intervention of grace is not to suggest there is an absence of "sorrow and failure: the possibility of these is necessary to the joy of deliverance." But this turning toward grace—or the hope thereof—is "a fleeting glimpse of Joy, Joy beyond the walls of the world, poignant as grief."[10]

Grace, after all, is a gift freely given, a sharing in God's mercy, compassion, and love. Like a flock of enormous eagles suddenly there to save the day, or a sorcerer who appears from nowhere to momentarily hold back the advancing darkness, the gift of grace arrives quite unexpectedly. But then the narrative reins are handed back to our heroes—back to us—and we continue on.

This isn't just fiction; this is God at work in our real lives! The Holy Spirit intervenes when we least expect it. How will we rise to the moment? How will we collaborate with grace when it touches us in our stories? Too often, our language for the spiritual fails us; we get bogged down in religious dogma, assumptions, and assignments that we think we understand—or at least, should pretend to understand. Our spiritual lives are reduced to half-hearted lessons, poorly memorized lines, and forgotten catechesis. Consequently, our spiritual journeys falter. We miss the moment of grace.

Maybe that's why I turn again and again to the fantastical as fuel for the spiritual journey, as a way to conjure raw material for the imagination, as a gateway into a much-needed retreat of grace and self-discovery.

C. S. Lewis did the same: "Why did one find it so hard to feel as one was told one ought to feel about God or about the sufferings of Christ? I thought the chief reason was that one was told one ought to. An obligation to feel can freeze feelings." He goes on: "The whole subject [of faith] was associated with lowered voices; almost as if it were something medical. But supposing that by casting all these things into an imaginary world, stripping them of their stained-glass and Sunday school association, one could make them for the first time appear in their real potency?"[11]

And so, in these pages, we set out to cast our ordinary lives into an imaginary world so as to wrestle with the power and potential of our quite extraordinary selves. The speculative meets the spiritual because I believe *praying* with these stories—in fact, putting ourselves into the stories and allowing those fantastical motifs to saturate our own daily joys and sorrows—will prove transformative.

"Far from being untruths, myths have traditionally been forefront in the shaping of human beings," writes renowned mythographer and Christian thinker Martin Shaw. "They show us what to defend, what to care about, the need for pluck, sacrifice, and generosity. In the writ-largeness of their narratives we can locate our own stories, like a river finding the sea."[12] Shaw is convinced that myths are meant to mature us, to make us more fully human.

Are we creating new myths? Or are we remembering the fantastical that has always been waiting within us? I believe it's the latter. And I believe that by spending time pondering these fantastical tropes, we better understand both who we are and whose we are. We discover our own stories, and we discover the Great Storyteller.

Who was the first person to dream up a fairy? I can't say. But I can say that the same mythic raw material exists in our own lives, that these creatures of legend and tales of old continue to matter because they continue to reflect deep truths about who we are, and where we're headed.

CHAPTER TWO

The Spirituality of Worldbuilding

Before undertaking a journey, it's wise to have a sense of the world you're stepping into. And so, let us take time to develop a spiritual practice that allows us to really *see* the world glimmering around us, and to glimpse what lies beyond. By understanding worldbuilding as a spiritual practice that is aligned with and augmented by a Catholic imagination, we will better grasp how fantastical worlds can help us more deeply enter our own.

The very first page—better still, the very first paragraph—of any speculative story answers the question, "What sort of world is this?" We look for clues. Is magic at work? Are monsters on the loose? Has a spaceship just taken off over the horizon? By understanding the world, we begin to understand the story and why it matters to our characters. Worldbuilding sets the stage and the stakes.

Worldbuilding in speculative storytelling is exactly what it sounds like: The storyteller quite literally needs to *build* a new and believable *world.* It's the process of plotting historical events, new languages, forgotten lore, socioeconomic patterns, and geographic wonders. It's the construction of a place that could be real if our imagination is given enough raw material with which to work. It's the making of new context and meaning in a landscape unique and wonderful and different—even if only in small, nuanced ways—from our own.

In her introduction to *The Book of the New Sun* series, historian Ada Palmer says this about wading through the dense worldbuilding of renowned Catholic speculative-fiction author Gene Wolfe:

> Reading for world-building requires retaining information without context: a term, a place, a coin, a category comes up once and we know what that is—a puzzle piece—that our task is to gather up these pieces as the author drops them, and to slowly assemble the whole. This is not easy. . . . To retain puzzle pieces that don't connect, dropped without context, is a skill that not all have. All had it once: it is how children read . . . trusting that they will connect to something someday.[13]

Her insights are important: We may hear in her words echoes of the spiritual life. After all, aren't we each going through our lives collecting these same puzzle pieces, able to make sense of them only once we've acquired additional context? Aren't we always trying to make meaning out of things big and small in our own days?

We glimpse, too, why children take to fairy tales and the fantastical so much more readily than many adults: Children are used to experiencing new worlds because our own world is still so new to them. Indeed, we might remind ourselves of the words of Jesus, who, in prayer, reflects that God has "hidden these things from the wise and the learned" but has "revealed them to the childlike."[14] We pray, then, for that childlike wonder as we journey through these pages, knowing how truly vast God's creation—God's own worldbuilding—is.

Worldbuilding can be seen as a deeply spiritual act. When we're looking at fantastical stories, we might be talking about literal new worlds such as Narnia, Middle-earth, Westeros, or Pandora. These stories might take place on a completely different planet than Earth, one that is infused with the power of magical gnomes. Or they might be set in a neighborhood not unlike the ones we live in, except that things are a little . . . off. Like a script from *The Twilight Zone* or *Black Mirror.* You're not simply assembling pieces of a structure. You're imbuing each piece with significance, with meaning; each piece points to something else, something larger, even if that something is out of view. Worldbuilding means constructing a place more expansive than you'll ever know and then inviting others to explore it. Worldbuilding means settling into a sacramental imagination, one that sees all things as pointing beyond themselves to a greater Source.

The very act of engaging with a work of science fiction, fantasy, horror, or some other speculative genre means the suspension of belief in what is—what we know and expect from our own lived experiences. And that means the reader or viewer must then be observant. Any detail or stray scrap of information becomes essential to understanding this new world and this new way of being and relating. Any object, conversation, or glimmer of new context is to be considered a valuable piece to that ultimate, enormous puzzle. These are windows into meaning and mystery and a deeper understanding of how this strange new world works. The truly gifted storyteller doesn't allow a single aspect to go to waste. Everything points to the larger story, with the enormity of the whole world potentially bound up in a solitary detail.

For me, this makes sense. It makes sense because I am a Catholic steeped in Ignatian spirituality. What does it mean to be Ignatian? Following in the footsteps of St. Ignatius of Loyola, it means that God is, and can be found, in all things. Of *course* every detail matters! If we look closely enough, every detail of our lives is revelatory of God.

This is the sacramental imagination at work: We believe that the raw material of creation can pierce the veil between this world and the supernatural, each thing pointing beyond itself toward God who made all things, and through those things, God's grace is manifested.

We already met Fr. Andrew Greeley. Here, again, we turn to his classic sociological text *The Catholic Imagination* in which he writes that it is our "religious sensibility which inclines Catholics to see the Holy lurking in creation," and that we're inclined to believe "the objects, events, and persons of daily life are revelations of grace."[15] Catholics, he says, live in an enchanted world, a point of view famously echoed by Jesuit poet Gerard Manley Hopkins, who says in his aptly named poem "God's Grandeur" that "The world is charged with the grandeur of God."[16]

I don't think you have to be Catholic, though, to appreciate this religious imagination, or even to engage in it. I extend to you the same spiritual invitation to participate in the process of world-building each day. We necessarily do so in our own nitty-gritty, ordinary lives just as much as in the speculative works we read and watch.

Why bother engaging this spiritual disposition of worldbuilding in our everyday lives? Because God continues to create. God invites us into the work of creation. Mystery continues to unfold around us, drawing us in so as to send us out. But too often we don't have eyes to see the Spirit at work. We know our wardrobe in our bedroom is no portal to Narnia. We walk the streets of Baltimore, Toronto, London, and Madrid, not those of Westeros. And so we see what we expect, and we expect to see what we've seen before.

But ours is a God of surprises beyond our expectations, delighting in creation that is yet to unfold. What if we spent our days in wonder, awe, and delight at the details we think we know so well? Rather than see them as we expect them to be, what if we saw them as small puzzle pieces that when pieced together reveal something greater, something spectacular about God and God's dream for us and our world? What if we allowed ourselves to be moved by these tiny details to dream up something new, something wonderful, something unpredictable?

What if we truly recognized God present in all things—and responded? Would we build a new, *better* world?

Would we be all the more enchanted by the one unfolding all around us?[17] I think we would.

As we begin this book of meditations on the speculative and the spiritual, we turn to four practices that will ground our spirituality of worldbuilding: trust your imagination; sink into specificity; see our world as grace-filled; and turn to wonder and awe.

WORLDBUILDING SPIRITUAL PRACTICE #1: TRUST YOUR IMAGINATION.

St. Ignatius of Loyola, for whom Ignatian spirituality is named, was a soldier long before he became a saint. Grievously wounded in battle, he was forced to spend months recovering in his home in Loyola, Spain, bedridden. It was there that his imagination ran wild. He dreamed of returning to a life of wooing women and waging war, but he took notice when those predictable dreams left him feeling hollow, empty, unsatisfied. He then turned to reading books on saints and the life of Christ. He slipped into a newly imagined world in which he saw himself living the life of a saint. Here, he felt consolation; he felt energized, affirmed, and as though he was being called to something greater.

It was through this exercise in imaginative prayer that God spoke to Ignatius. Ignatius opened himself up to the Spirit at work and through that openness discerned his life's calling. When he imagined himself as a pilgrim, someone living for God, he was enlivened. He became desolate when he imagined anything else. It was in the imagination that God spoke most clearly to Ignatius, and he was able to dream up a new, more purpose-driven way of life for himself.

But that's not all. Ignatius went on, through his own life of prayer and reflection, to write the *Spiritual Exercises*, which consist of a series of meditations on the life of Jesus and guided exercises to help retreatants discern their life's purpose. Because of his sickbed experience of God at work in the imagination, Ignatius realized that God was at work in the imagination of other people, too. And so, his Spiritual Exercises *require* that individuals who pray the retreat *imagine* themselves in the scenes of Scripture. They are told to place themselves in the story, to take on the role of a character, or to simply dream up a new character and role within the scene. This method of contemplative prayer is the backbone of the meditations you'll find in this book.

Ignatius insists that God is in all things and that the Spirit works in our imagination. This is why we can pray with fairy tales. This is why we can put ourselves in the stories and trust that God's Spirit will speak to us.

The imagination is an important tool of justice, too. We know our world is wounded and broken in so many ways. The status quo simply will not suffice. We need to *imagine* a better world. We need to look beyond the old rhythms and routines of life to fuel those dreams. "The imaginary is the mental realm in which the juxtaposing of new possibilities takes places," writes the late Fr. Robert J. Schreiter, CPPS, in his essay "The Catholic Social Imaginary and

Peacebuilding." He continues: "A Catholic imaginary sees the world filled with God's grace, even as sin and evil continue to be present."[18] Speculative storytelling is full of other worlds, from distant planets to mystical gardens, all wrestling with the collision between good and less-than-good. What can we learn from these magical places? Can we allow those reflections to feed our imagination and thus make better our own place here and now? How might the juxtaposing of the fantastical and the real allow us to dream up something new? These are the necessary questions that will guide us in the pages to come.

WORLDBUILING SPIRITUAL PRACTICE #2:
Sink into specificity.

Details are not simply important for building worlds; they are also essential for revealing what matters in these worlds. If God is present in these details, then we can say God is speaking to us through them. What is God trying to say to us through the very fabric of existence, regardless of whether that existence is imaginary or real?

In the Ignatian tradition, we talk about being contemplatives in action. This requires, in the words of Jesuit priest Walter J. Burghardt, taking a "long, loving look at the real."[19] We must look plainly and clearly at our world, our lives, ourselves. We must allow our hearts to be both broken and moved to joy by what we see.

It is in the details of our lives that the Spirit works, not in some vague amorphous amalgamation of what it means to be human. We are each unique and wonderfully made. Creation itself is singing, and its songs are revelatory of its Creator. Taking this long, loving look is in itself a prayer; in essence, we come to know God more intimately and, in so doing, come to know ourselves.

Indian Jesuit Anthony de Mello wrote in his book *Awareness* how easy it is for us to lump things together and thus miss the ordinary and the specific. He points to a sparrow, how marvelous a being it is to the mind of a child who has never before encountered such a creature. "The first time the child sees that fluffy, alive, moving object, and you say to him, 'Sparrow,' then tomorrow when the child sees another fluffy, moving object similar to it he says, 'Oh, sparrows. I've seen sparrows. I'm *bored* by sparrows.'"[20] The point here is that, in truth, each sparrow is unique. So, have we *really* seen *this* one? Have I allowed *this* one to speak to me, to move my heart? Ultimately, sinking into the specific and allowing ourselves to be moved should develop in us a disposition of gratitude to the One to whom these details ultimately point, as well as an increased awareness of how distinctly unique each thing truly is. Once more, we see the importance of a childlike approach to these puzzle pieces of life.

WORLDBUILDING SPIRITUAL PRACTICE #3:
See our world as grace-filled.

Fr. Greeley reminds us that we see "the Holy lurking in creation" and that all things are dripping with grace. God appears at any moment, and miracles abound. Our fortunes can and do change quite suddenly, with little rhyme or reason. And yet we persist all the same, perhaps because we must. We muddle onward in good times and in bad.

We are both always ready to receive grace and ever mindful that we must continue down the road regardless of whether we see the effects of grace. We know God can intervene. And yet, God desires to collaborate with us in all our unique specificity. Put another way and informed by the stories we love, it sure seems like magic should solve our problems. No doubt, magic does go a long way! And yet, ultimately, we—or our protagonist—must get across the finish line without it. We can't rely solely on outside forces to help us become who we are called to be; we must use what we have and who we are to complete the story. But when they appear, those outside forces change the narrative, giving us a much-needed boost.

As previously mentioned, Tolkien calls it the *eucatastrophe*, the sudden eruption of the good. The wizard in white appears on the hilltop to chase away the bloodthirsty hoards! The day is saved but it is not over. There is more work to be done, and we cannot assume that the wizard will always show up to reshuffle our fortunes. (He has other places to be, after all.) So, we get back to work.

Grace abounds. The world pulses with it. Miracles exist. And God does intervene. But we're not called to be puppets or playthings but rather collaborators and co-laborers, and that means we must do our part. We're given what we need to deepen our knowledge of self, vocation, and others. Grace is not a shortcut; it's a pathway.

What does this mean for worldbuilding? Look for grace everywhere; expect it everywhere. But don't be surprised if *you* become the instrument of salvation.

WORLDBUILDING SPIRITUAL PRACTICE #4:
Turn to wonder and awe.

We develop a disposition of curiosity, which allows us to delight in the world around us, when we cultivate a point of view that embraces wonder and awe. "We all like astonishing tales because they touch the nerve of the ancient instinct of astonishment," the great English writer G. K. Chesterton says. "This is proved by the fact that when we are very young children, we do not need fairy tales: we only need tales. Mere life is interesting enough."[21] We are drawn to the unknowable, to that which wows and amazes us.

These other worlds of speculative storytelling can do exactly that. But so too is the world we live in deserving of wonder and awe. Think of the sparrows. Think of how little we really know about things. And think of that muscle of curiosity that we would do well to nourish if we are to feed our imaginations and continue to build a world worthy of wonder and awe.

When I was a child learning about the Gifts of the Holy Spirit, I always stumbled on the final one: Fear of the Lord. As I've aged, I've learned that it is better articulated as wonder and awe. We aren't supposed to cower before God; rather, we turn in astonishment at the unfolding mystery that is God's love. Creation is always greater; the world is always bigger; the story is always expanding. God's worldbuilding is worthy of wonder and awe because it is always so far beyond our knowing. God extends an invitation: *Come and see*. Our spirituality of worldbuilding means we must step into the vastness of God's creation, prepared to be surprised and delighted and challenged.

Step into the unknown.

Stories of fantasy and myth invite us into a place of mystery and wonder. We step into an enchanted forest or an unknown realm. Who knows what might be beyond that wardrobe's door or down that uncanny rabbit hole? We are prepared to have all our assumptions and preconceived notions about ourselves and our world challenged.

We do this in our real lives, too, though perhaps in less dramatic fashion. We step into a new job or a new role, becoming a parent or a manager, the citizen of a new country or a neighbor on a new street. How wondrous would it be if, in these seemingly mundane moments, we brought with us an eye for enchantment?

God is there, I believe, in that hidden forest, in that glimmering cave. God is beckoning us to step out and into the unknown, to allow ourselves to be surprised by the God of Surprises, to expect the impossible because miracles are indeed all around us. But these so-called miracles aren't just happening *out there*; God invites us into collaboration. Our hands can be the ones that bring such casual magic into the world if we but look for God's Spirit at work.

That's why, when we step out of our status quo, out of our comfortable and usual ways and into the enchanted forest, or that new job, or the haunted castle, or that invitation to be a kinder, more truthful person, we need a teacher. A mentor. A guide. We need someone to show us the way.

Too often, we look for these guides in our old lives. We expect someone who embodies our old status quo to teach us how to live in a totally new way. This is not only unfair, it is also unwise. Luke Skywalker needed Obi-Wan Kenobi to teach him the ways of a Jedi Knight; Uncle Owen was only ever going to teach him about moisture farming. Harry Potter needed Hagrid to bust through that door and introduce him to the wizarding ways; his aunt and uncle were never going to be brave enough to do so. Dorothy needed Glinda, and Bilbo needed Gandalf, and Katniss needed Haymitch.

All of these mentor figures come from the other side of the status quo. These are figures who, by their very nature, by their very stories, embody what it means to transcend the usual way of things.

We need such a figure. We look to Jesus Christ, God Incarnate, who comes to us quite literally from the other side of things. Christ shakes up the status quo and shows us how to walk a new way of life. He turns things upside down—the blind see, the sinners are embraced, and all are welcome—and shows us a new way of living.

This is an uncomfortable invitation, and that's the downside of the enchanted forest: There are things in there that make us squirm. We avoid discomfort. Being a Jedi is hard. Same with being a wizard. If we welcome the sinners, then whom can we despise? How can we feel good about ourselves if everyone is good? How can we make sense of this completely new way of living?

This is a key moment in our stories. This is the ritual of initiation. We step out into the unknown to confront what is uncomfortable so as to return transformed. Cultures the world over were built upon such customs; it's no surprise then that we see the pattern in mythmaking, too. Martin Shaw breaks this necessary trajectory into three stages: Severance, Threshold, and Return. We can only cross the threshold into the unknown if we sever the ties that keep us bound to the comfortable and serene. This is hard work; we don't want to do it. But if we don't answer the call, the quest never begins and transformation becomes all but impossible. The story of Bilbo Baggins lands quite differently if he never leaves the Shire. "We have a cozy, cookie-cutter, one-size-fits-all, long-entrenched, batten-down-the-hatches belief. But what can happen with that?" Shaw asks, and then answers, "I don't know how we get much in the way of Holy Spirit if we never set out to begin with."[22] If we want more, if we want to learn who we can become, then we have to take a risk. And if we take that risk, if we step into the wild and find ourselves, then we return to our community with something to give.

Jessica Brody, in her book on novel writing, *Save the Cat! Writes A Novel*, reminds us that this transformative work often happens in the second act of most stories. This is when the protagonist enters what she calls the upside-down world.[23] Everything is unlike what we expect and we are necessarily tested. We see our weaknesses in new light, but so too do we better understand our strengths. It is from this upside-down world that our hoped-for mentors come, the ones who know how to survive in this new and uncertain way of being. The upside-down quite literally flips the status quo on its head. And what we thought we knew about how the world works is tested. This is a good thing. It is here that we are transformed.

Jesuit priest Ryan Duns wrote a book called *Theology of Horror: The Hidden Depths of Popular Films*. I interviewed him about it for a weekly podcast, *AMDG: A Jesuit Podcast*. We talked about horror films, of course, and what they might teach us about God and our spiritual lives.

Fr. Duns was keen to lay out the plot beats of a monster movie. The monster appears, we know, and throws everything into disarray. The very presence of the monster challenges the status quo because suddenly we must rethink not only what's real and possible but also our place in the world. If monsters exist, then should we be living differently? The whole plot of a monster movie is to kill the monster. We want to go back to the way things were before our stories were so grossly interrupted. We want to pretend such frightening things do not occur in our comfortable corner of creation.

Jesus is the monster, Fr. Duns said. We tame him, kill him, and pretend he was never here disrupting our lives. Jesus breaks through our status quo, and we don't necessarily like what we see or what we're invited to become. But this is not God's way. God is not content to leave us in our status quo. God is not content to leave the world as it is. God desires that we dream bigger, and God invites us into that dream.

Jesus Christ is both mentor and monster, guide and disruptor. Jesus shows us the way—he quite literally *is* the Way—but he also unsettles the path so that we may see more clearly the foundation upon which we walk. Why? Because we need to get up and be about God's business. We need to find the courage to step into the unknown. We need to allow ourselves to see the enchanted possibilities lying just below the surface to be rid of the rusted old infrastructure that is holding us and our world back.

In *Star Wars: Episode IV—A New Hope*, aboard the Millennium Falcon, Luke Skywalker begins to feel the flow of the Force within him. He's excited. "Hokey religions and ancient weapons are no match for a good blaster at your side," says Han Solo. Luke feels dejected. But his mentor, the old Jedi Knight Obi-Wan Kenobi, is undeterred. "You've taken your first steps into a larger world," he insists. In short, the interior spiritual movement at work within Luke is necessarily interwoven with the visible flow of ordinary events taking place in the wider universe, even if Han can't see it. Luke is connected to the ever-evolving world around him. But these are only first steps.

So, too, for us. Our own stories are single blocks in the great myth God is constructing. But we cannot grow complacent. Our story continues to unfold. As it does, let us look for God's hand in details big and small. Let us be prepared to be surprised. Let us see how we will be tested, and in what way we may be asked to contribute to building the world God desires.

CHAPTER THREE

The Art of Rereading and Contemplation

Gene Wolfe's sprawling four-part saga *The Book of the New Sun* is thick, both because of its number of pages and because of the complexity of its wildly winding plot. It's not the sort of book you randomly pick up at the bookstore and take to the beach. Wolfe, one of the great American science-fiction and fantasy authors of the twentieth century, was a committed Catholic. It was this intersection of Catholicism and the fantastical that originally drew me to his work, though once I held his intimidating tomes in my hands, I grew a bit apprehensive.

"The Book of the New Sun is cluttered with more than spaceships, species, and ruins," writes author and historian Ada Palmer in the volume's introductory essay, "The Path of the New Sun." "It is cluttered with characters who come and go abruptly without closure, their functions clear only with rereading and contemplation."[24]

Rereading? I thought. *I can barely get through these books once; I'm expected to read them again to understand what's going on!?* That's quite a tall order for any author to make of their readers. And yet, I do believe that this invitation to *reread* and *contemplate* the stories of our lives—stories based on and built up by the kind of unfolding worldbuilding Wolfe was known for and that we have been reflecting on—is in line with our Catholic speculative imagination.

In fact, this is the heart of prayer: We turn to God repeatedly, trying to understand how God's Spirit has been at work in our lives. The daily prayer attributed to St. Ignatius of Loyola, the Examen, asks us to do exactly this: Review our day in gratitude and, in the company of God, discover the small, seemingly innocuous details that are revelatory of God's grace in our lives. We *need* to return to our stories to find the patterns through which God is unfolding. And we must do so in a contemplative matter, making ourselves open and available to the surprise of God's abiding presence.

To that end, you may want to pause on, circle back to, or reread multiple times certain contemplations in this book. Perhaps one really speaks to you; if so, God may be inviting you to contemplate the fruits of that contemplation once more. Perhaps a different contemplation leaves you feeling dry; this, too, may be an invitation to return with fresh curiosity. Indeed, the adventure of our lives continues, and you may find that beginning this book anew brings novel insights to your story. After all, every time you approach one of these chapters or contemplations—just as every time you sit in prayer—you are a new and changed person, even if ever so slightly. You are always growing.

When I made the Spiritual Exercises of St. Ignatius of Loyola, my spiritual director was keen on ensuring that I received the graces asked for. Each module of the Exercises invites retreatants to ask for a specific grace, and it is the responsibility of the director to help retreatants realize when those graces have been received. The director has the purview to insist on the repetition of a module until the graces asked for have been realized. This is delicate work, more art than science, but it is representative of the kind of accompaniment we each need in the spiritual life: We need companions who can help us recognize and name those good gifts God desires to give us. We also need companions who can help us persevere through a particular moment, to sink into an experience so as not to miss what God desires to accomplish in our lives. And so, I repeated a few modules week after week until my director was sure I'd realized and received those good graces God was giving me.

Repetition isn't a punishment, nor does it reflect some intrinsic failure to fully grasp a concept the first time around. When we're talking about prayer, we're talking about a constant dwelling in God's Spirit, a labyrinthine walk into grace that at times appears redundant until we reach the end and realize that every step was essential. Sometimes that looks like the simple act of waiting: waiting on God's vision to manifest itself. We do so not because some sudden bout of grace or spiritual understanding will solve all of our problems but because we know the spiritual life is about trajectory setting. Each grace received, each encounter with God, slowly directs our lives. We savor these moments; we desire more of them. We put ourselves along the path upon which we might most readily find them again.

These are sacred building blocks with which we build the road into our deepest selves. Once we've laid one stone, the next one becomes all the more clear. But we need to go slowly; we need to place these stones in their proper location. And that means pausing, sitting with, and contemplating God's many graces. That means resisting the temptation to rush ahead and being courageous enough to walk the path anew. We circle back not because we wish to rewrite a finished story or dwell solely in the past but because walking even the most well-trod road grants new insights.

An Irish Jesuit friend of mine walks the Camino de Santiago nearly every year. It's an ancient pilgrimage through northern Spain. He does so not because he has forgotten the way and needs a reminder or because he is trying to fix a mistaken pilgrimage of the past. He's not chasing some *perfect* pilgrimage; no such thing exists. He does it because each passage brings new insight, new graces, new revelations. Repetition is essential to our spiritual journeys.

Palmer, in that same essay, says this of Gene Wolfe's work: "[He] who warns us in each volume that this road (like Dante's) is no easy one, asks us to trust that this mess of strangers, interruptions, tangents and abortive missions, with no resolution at volume's end, will mean something."[25] This sounds like life to me! A mess of people, places, and things that seem random and scattered until we take the time to *reread* our stories and *contemplate* how God might be at work.

Whether embarking upon or ending our journey, this invitation to reflect on the strangers we encounter in our life stories is an important one. Jesus himself reminds us that Christ is present in all people and in all places, and that whatever we do for the least of God's people we do for Christ. In all these strangers, then, in all these seemingly random, muddled characters that appear in our lives and feature in our stories, we should be seeing Christ alive.

I remember being particularly struck by an insight into Tolkien's work. Contrary to C. S. Lewis, who, in the character of Aslan, painted a rather clear Christlike character, Tolkien's world refuses easy Jesus parallels. This is good; this is helpful. When we look to identify the "Jesus character" in a story, we run the risk of negating an oh-so-necessary Christian truth: Christ is in all characters.

Tolkien, then, helps us. Who is the so-called "Jesus character" in Middle-earth? Is it the wizard Gandalf? Certainly, he has the qualities of a teaching hero, and he quite literally rises from the dead. Is it Aragorn? Here is the would-be king trying to bring about a new kingdom of peace and justice amid a land of darkness and shadow. Is it Frodo? Jesus, after all, is meek, nonviolent, and hidden in the most vulnerable among us. We could go on, but the point is clear: We are not called to find Jesus in a single character; we are called to see Christ present in everyone, *just as we are called to do in our real lives.* We are called to realize that to be Christlike is to be many things and that there are many roads to Christlike living.

We glimpse something of this Christlike nature in Tolkien's description of the Istari, the wizards: "It is said indeed that being embodied the Istari had need to learn much anew by slow experience, and though they knew whence they came the memory of the Blessed Realm was to them a vision from afar off, for which (so long as they remained true to their mission) they yearned exceedingly."[26] This description captures well the wizards; it reminds us of Christ. But it also points to us and our own daily efforts to realize God's dream.

Who, then, is Christ in your story? Ah! The answer is everyone. But as you reread and contemplate your own life, I wonder if you don't see Jesus appearing in new people, in new places. Maybe the better questions are, *Who is Jesus this time around?* and *How is Jesus at work in you right now?*

I wonder: As we discover Christ alive within us, how is our God of surprises inviting us to share that *eucatastrophic grace* with others? "For the whole law is fulfilled in one statement, namely, 'You shall love your neighbor as yourself.'"[27] So, let's get to it.

PART II

The Adventure

And now begins our contemplative adventure. The road ahead is not an academic exercise. You will be asked to place yourself in these scenes, to conjure from your own ordinary life something fantastical. Recall that each contemplation begins and ends with an immersive experience drawn from the ethos of high fantasy. Nestled within these contemplations are brief essays that draw your attention to the supernatural wonders already unfolding in your daily existence. Key to it all is your imagination—let it roam free. Allow God's Spirit to work therein, revealing, through your imaginative muscles, new insight into God's dream for you and for the world.

THE FIRST CONTEMPLATION

The Wizard, or, The One Who Issues the Call

Step into adventure.

He's tall and cloaked from head to toe, wrapped in the deepest blues. He's also quite unexpected. There's an aura about him that you don't entirely trust, though his wizened face is smiling down upon you through a graying beard and deep wrinkles, gentle and kind. In his left hand he holds a tall, gnarled staff. His other, he extends toward you, outstretched, welcoming.

But you don't trust it. You don't trust him—this stranger from a foreign land, all cloaks and staffs and uncertainty. You shouldn't have opened the door, late as it is. You never open the door for strangers, certainly not after the sun has set. And so you stand there on your porch shaking your head. You're not quite sure why. Are you disagreeing with something the man said? Or could it be that you are scolding yourself for having stumbled into the possibility of the unknown?

The stranger knows your name. He speaks it. His voice is soft, inviting, but also firm. "Come along," he says. "There are things I'd like to show you before you set off."

"I'm not going anywhere," you say, the words tumbling out of your mouth. "It's late and I've a busy day tomorrow and besides I've just made myself a cup of chamomile tea, which I expect has gone quite cold by now." You frown, shake your head again. And that's that, you think to yourself.

But the strange man on your porch chuckles lightly, smiles more brightly. "I expect you're right," he says. "And I expect it will stay that way." He nods to himself, shifting his grip on the staff. "And what's more, I expect you'll have to get used to a great many things far more discomforting than a cold cup of chamomile tea."

He turns to face the starry night. You follow his gaze despite your desire to flee back inside, to bury your head in your pillow and ignore the odd feeling of wonder that is coming over you. Was that a shooting star? A cluster of dancing lightning bugs? Or something more? The sky is full of mystery, you think.

"The world is full of mystery, my friend," the man says, turning back to you, reading your mind. Again, he extends his hand toward you. "But you'll not find it if you refuse to step into it."

And with that, the man leaps from your porch to the ground. A blue light emanates from the staff. He disappears into the darkness but the glow of the blue light lingers, floating in his wake.

You wonder: Should I follow the wizard into the unknown?

Turn to the ordinary.

"The man's a wizard. I don't know how he does it."

My friend was describing my long-time spiritual director, the late Jesuit priest Jim Bowler. My friend had just had his own first experience of spiritual direction with Jim and was shocked.

"It's like he knew what I was going to say before I said it."

I smiled and nodded. I'd had plenty of similar experiences with Jim. It seemed he could speak to your soul, point to the Spirit at work therein, and then draw you forth, newly energized to go out and do good in the world. This is the goal of spiritual direction: A good director accompanies you in the spiritual life, helping you identify God already at work in your day. The director doesn't make decisions for you; they simply listen and then reflect back to you what they've heard. More to the point, they reflect what they've heard of God already at work within you.

Jim was particularly gifted in the art of spiritual direction. But he was no wizard. He couldn't divine the future or summon blue flames or levitate. He was simply a good listener who had spent many years in prayer, study, and practice. To my mind, Jim came from the other side of the spiritual life. His insights seemed so profound because they always came from another place, a place I had yet to reach. A place I could not yet fully imagine but was determined to find. And yet there he was, sitting in a chair across the room, pointing the way. He believed in me. He believed I could get there. He believed I had something to offer the world. And so, together, we discovered whether his beliefs were well placed.

It's not always a wizard who shows up to jump-start adventure. Sometimes it's an enchantress who descends from the sky, or a frog that leaps in through the window. The invitation can come by mail or via puffs of smoke. The old-man-with-a-white-beard motif is but one of many gateways into the unknown. The key is that last bit: *We are being invited to step beyond our status quo.* The challenge comes from the other side of things.

Pause for a moment and reflect on your status quo. Where are you in your life right now? Is it where you want to be? Are you fully alive, realizing your fullest potential? Perhaps you are; perhaps you are doing great things in the world. If so, good for you! Even so, we never want to become complacent. We never want to cease dreaming up the impossible. We never want the flame that fuels our desire for adventure, for *more*, to burn out. Our own unique vocation in this life is constantly unfolding, and so it is incumbent upon us to make ourselves available to receive invitations to adventure whenever they are extended. They come to us, arriving over and over again, sometimes when they are least expected. We have to be ready to be surprised. We have to be prepared to meet our own wizard in whatever guise our wizards take.

Why this readiness?

The wizard invites us into mystery and points the way. It's not the conjuring of cheap tricks that makes a wizard; the magic is there to remind us that we're dealing with something or someone we don't fully understand. And that makes us curious as well as uncomfortable, both of which are good things. Curiosity beckons us forward; discomfort prods us to keep going. We are propelled by a desire to know: Where has this proverbial magician come from? What does he know that we don't? What life experiences have led him to this time, to this place, to *me*?

In truth, that's what spiritual direction is. Jim only ever had a handful of suggestions and a few concrete pieces of text to refer to. When all is said and done, Jim knew that the primary guide was the Spirit at work within me.

So it is for you, too. Your path is necessarily different than mine, but what we have in common is that we all need a guide to show us the way. Be on the lookout for your own wizard, your own spiritual companion. Who is that person who represents the other side of your current status quo? Who can usher you into an upside-down world where what you believe to be true about yourself and your place in society can be reimagined? In that place of discomfort, and with a disposition of curiosity, inevitably we begin to see more clearly. Stripped of what we know (or thought we knew), the field opens up to reveal what was hidden, what needs to be seen, and what we are uniquely positioned to offer the world.

Because ultimately it's not about where our feet may lead us, it's about what we find within. This, perhaps, is the most significant gift of so-called wizards: It is their ability to see something within us that we hardly knew existed at all.

And now, cross the threshold that links the ordinary to the fantastical.

The blue light is still hanging above the pathway leading from your home. You think of the mysterious man who vanished into shadow and darkness. You think of how little you know about him, about where he's come from, where he's going. You think of your friends, your colleagues, your neighbors, your family. These are people you know. These are the people who know you. They bring you great comfort.

And yet . . .

You realize they don't have the answer to the mystery that is seemingly unfurling at your very feet. How could they? They don't know the stranger who just vanished into the night. And they've never been along the road that stretches before you. No one has. This is your road.

There is only one who knows where it may lead: the very stranger who has just set out upon it. Your decision, you realize, comes down to this: Will you follow after mystery, or will you sit in the known and comfortable?

You lace up your boots, you lock your door, and you leave behind your tea. The wizard was right: Cold tea is the least of the discomforts to come.

Wizards appear to call us from comfort, point us instead to the land beyond. How reticent are we to welcome them?

THE SECOND CONTEMPLATION

The Walking Stick, or, The Tool That Keeps Us Going

Step into adventure.

The puzzling stranger has left a walking stick leaning against your door. You wonder if he did that on purpose. The man didn't seem like one prone to forgetfulness. You examine the stick, rubbing your fingers up and down over the rough wood. It's a bit ostentatious: Mysterious runes that seem to glow a dark purple line its blackened length.

"I can't bring this," you say aloud. "What will people think of me? That I'm some wanna-be magician on the loose out in the world? They'll think I've lost my mind." You'd feel like an imposter.

Even so, you hold the staff. You feel the weight of it in your hand. You rationalize. It is true that you could use a walking stick, even if something simpler would suffice. The road is long and winding and there are bound to be rough patches out there in the wild world.

You shake your head. You're thinking too hard. You don't need this silly thing.

Turn to the ordinary.

When I was younger and went for a walk in the woods, my eyes were always searching to find the perfect walking stick. When I found one, I'd pretend to be a wizard, of course, using my staff to cast spells and summon great powers straight from the ground. It was silly and entertaining but also seemingly necessary for a successful hike.

My daughters now do the same. They argue with one another over who found the better stick. They pretend as though they really need the help of their short staffs, as though they'd never be able to make it through the woods on just their own two feet.

At the end of every hike—and often to the girls' disappointment—we make sure to leave our staffs at the trailhead. We do this so that someone else can use these treasures to navigate the perilous path. We like to think of it as offering a helping hand from two little girls who've already made the journey. We're paying it forward.

We're also keeping our own front porch from becoming littered with tree parts.

The passing on of our so-called wizards' staffs is a handoff in some cosmic race, small tokens of goodwill from my family to yours. But what strikes me is this: We don't need those walking sticks—that is, until we *do*. When my wife and I hiked the Camino de Santiago, we relied on walking sticks that were actual hiking poles made of metal and rubber, not found tree limbs. Day after day we leaned heavily on those poles. These weren't fun, silly accessories but essential, helpful tools.

I thought of the wizard staffs I wielded as a child, and of the walking sticks my girls are so competitive about still. On the Camino de Santiago, my hiking pole was more than a tool; it was an object imbued with memory and story that I quite literally clung to each and every day, with each and every step. The cosmic hand-off had been from me to me, a game turned into a reality. I hadn't needed those walking sticks as a child, but I certainly needed that hiking pole as an adult walking the Camino. And my grandfather needed his walker, and my grandmother needed her cane, and on and on it goes. We think we're playing a game until suddenly we're playing at life. And we reach for a tool that we thought was a silly afterthought, only to realize that our very life depends on it.

I wonder if that's not the spiritual life, faith itself: a walking stick to support our journey in good times but especially in difficult ones. Something we find childish until we realize just how powerful such a tool really is. Something passed from one generation to the next. Something imbued with stories. Something shared between strangers.

Something that can be picked up and treasured.

* * *

AND NOW, CROSS THE THRESHOLD THAT LINKS THE ORDINARY TO THE FANTASTICAL.

The staff feels good in your hand; you're glad you brought it along. Perhaps you'll have an opportunity to return it to the mysterious stranger. Or maybe it's yours to keep. At any rate, you wonder about the stories it could tell. You wonder about the stories it will allow you to live.

You barely lean on it now, walking at a rapid clip. But the day may come when that stick will keep you upright, keep you going on the path that stretches before you. On that day, you'll be glad you took it along.

The staff keeps us upright and moving forward. How often do we leave it behind when we feel strong, and only remember its existence when we stumble?

THE THIRD CONTEMPLATION

The Company, or, The Friends You Need Along the Way

STEP INTO ADVENTURE.

Just up and along the road is a tavern you know; you can just make out its welcoming glow against the evening's lengthening shadows. The Duckkeeper's Brewd—a punny name. You laugh in spite of yourself. And the laughter helps your nerves, though not half as well as your usual cup of deep brown ale. You pick up the pace, stretching your strides as far as they might go, trying not to linger too long with your thoughts in the darkness.

You wonder if the usual crew will be there. You can picture their faces, hear their raucous conversation, see the twinkle in their eyes. You've been friends with some of these folks for a very long time. They know all about your past and your hopes for the future. And you know their stories, too. Just thinking of these familiar faces brings a smile to your own.

Then you begin to muse about what they will think of this adventure you're on. Will they mock you? Scold you? Try to convince you of your foolishness? Will your quest for something more somehow weaken the ties you have with these friends?

You trudge up the tavern's stone stairs, clutching your walking stick tighter with every step. You know you can't linger; if you do, you might never leave at all. But one drink shared with friends won't derail your adventure, and then you'll get a few hours of rest at the inn.

You push the tavern door open and revel in the warm air that washes over you, the familiar sounds of comforting conversation. You step inside.

Turn to the ordinary.

There are many ways to be a friend.

There are friends who are always there, always present to our joys and suffering. There are friends who send a handwritten note "just because," and who always remember our birthday with a colorful card. There are friends who are good at listening and those who are great at building us up with their words. There are friends who help us move from one dorm room or apartment or rental or home to another. There are friends who visit us in the hospital and friends who ask about our aging parents. There are friends with whom we get a drink once a week and friends with whom we schedule a monthly lunch and there are friends we look forward to seeing at book club and on the soccer field.

And then there are friends we don't see and don't hear from. They fade from our memory but, due to any number of those delightful twists in life's road, suddenly find their way back to us. These friends we pick right back up with as though the years haven't passed.

I spend a great deal of time reflecting on the kind of friend that I am. I hope that I inhabit the following qualities: I want to be there for people, to be counted upon, to be trusted with the intimate details of a friend's own story. But sometimes the waves of life crash down with little warning, and suddenly days and weeks and months have passed and we never did get around to scheduling that lunch.

And so I take some solace in that final kind of friend who, like leaves dancing on a hidden breeze, skitters in and out of our lives—sudden, sharp colors of falling beauty. In truth, we are all called to be this kind of friend, the one who appears quite suddenly and who may depart just as unexpectedly. Life carries us away as time marches on, but the memories—brief, intense, beloved—remain with us. Can we honor them? Can we return to them? Can we treasure them once more, together, if given the opportunity?

In the Catholic tradition, we speak of the communion of saints, a holy potluck of folks we know inside and out as well as strangers we've only heard mentioned in passing. These are the folks who have lived good and holy lives, whose example we seek to learn from, even emulate. We can't pray with each of these saints every day; there's simply not enough time! But as the seasons of our life turn, we may find a different one of these holy friends suddenly stopping at our doorstep. Perhaps they stay awhile; perhaps they vanish quickly into the night. But they bring something with them, something we learn from, something to be honored in their own stories.

We, too, bring with us treasured insights and unique experiences. We offer them freely both to our friends and to those strangers we may, in time, call by that other name. But then, when life calls us once more, we stand and say our goodbyes and set off on the path. Why?

Because we are all part of that communion of saints. We are all in holy company. But we can appreciate one another's holiness only if we share our stories and treasure the stories that have been entrusted to us. That's the work of a moment; that's the work of a lifetime.

✷✷✷

AND NOW, CROSS THE THRESHOLD THAT LINKS THE ORDINARY TO THE FANTASTICAL.

The Duckkeeper's Brewd is quiet tonight. Your friends aren't here; your usual booth is empty. You slide in all the same, imagining where each person would normally sit. Even just the memory brings a smile, though one tinged with sadness.

"The usual?" the old barkeep calls.

"Aye," you call back. You can't help but wonder if your usual is about to change irreparably. You wanted to see those familiar faces; you wanted to feel the comfort of their presence. But now you wonder if what you really wanted was an excuse to stay.

The barkeep sets down the glass; a bit of brown liquid spills onto the table. He wipes it with his napkin. "You'd think I'd learn by now," he says, chuckling as he walks off.

You drink your ale quickly, stand, settle your bill. "Let them know I was here," you say, catching the barkeep's eye and deciding to forgo the comfort and warmth of a room at the inn. "And let them know I'll be gone for a while." The old man nods. "But I'll be back," you add. "I think."

The barkeep shrugs. "We'll see you when we see you. Bring us back something nice." He winks.

Companions journey with us,
even if only in memory.
How do we honor the stories others
have entrusted to us?

THE FOURTH CONTEMPLATION

The Magic Stones, or, The Reminder That There's More Than Meets the Eye

Step into adventure.

You hadn't meant to linger. You really needed to be moving along. But the bazaar at the edge of town swept you up in its pungent smells and friendly chatter and shiny wares. It couldn't hurt to stop and look, right? It couldn't hurt to see what the traders had brought to market today. And now here you are, caught up in a conversation you hadn't sought over goods you don't need.

"Those are magic, you know," the man says. "You've got a good eye—and good luck. I only found those yesterday." He smiles, revealing a mouth with more golden implants than original teeth. He runs his hand through a long, graying beard, as though thinking. "I'm a reasonable man. I'm sure we can agree on a reasonable price."

You lean heavily on your walking stick, shift the weight of the pack on your back. You shrug, pretending indifference. You glance at other goods on the table in front of you, trying to avoid the man's prying eyes.

In truth, you're irritated that the man caught you. You had indeed been looking longingly at the stones. There are three of them: one purple, one turquoise, and one yellow. They sit, unassuming, in a pile atop a small leather pouch. There was really no reason they should have captured your attention. There was no reason this man and his flimsy market stall should have caused you to stop—his was one of dozens. And yet, here you are, caught in the man's stare, enchanted by a handful of colorful rocks.

"Magic?" you say. "What kind of magic?"

"The kind of magic you need," the man replies. His words sit squarely at the intersection of intriguing and unhelpful, and you roll your eyes. "I'll have other buyers," he says in response. "But I can see they're calling to you. That could be the magic, eh?"

You sigh. You reach into your pocket. "How much?" you ask. The man smiles again. And you feel like a fool.

Turn to the ordinary.

I promised my girls they could choose a souvenir at the Renaissance Faire. My youngest quickly took me up on the offer, rushing into the nearest artisan shop as though the place was about to go out of business. I was suddenly out twenty bucks, and she was the proud owner of a pair of genuine fairy wings. My youngest was very happy.

My oldest was more discerning. Slowly, painstakingly, we perused the shops. At each stop, I had to review the budget—"No, just twenty dollars"—and my commitment—"Yes, I'm sure. That's what your sister got." We were drifting away from a fun perusal of medieval wares into the dangerous territory of "Just buy something already; we're not here for the trinkets."

We stumbled upon an attraction where they let you mine for gemstones. In reality what they do is hand you a bag full of sand and colorful rocks, and you pour the bag over a colander and hose it down using the water in the wooden piping contraption.

My girls love gemstones. And we stood gawking at the contraption long enough to draw the attention of the lady working at the booth.

"Are you princesses interested in searching for magical gemstones?" she asked. At that point I knew my money was basically in that lady's pocket, so I staunched the bleeding and simply said, "Let's go with the ten-dollar option."

My oldest held that bag of rocks in her hand like she was holding a baby bird. Carefully, carefully, she cleaned those colorful rocks. We gasped at their shine; we were dazzled by their glow.

"My goodness," the lady said. "These are so rare. So precious! You can see here"—she pointed to some indecipherable detail—"that they're very old. Ancient. And you, little princess, are the first person to ever touch them, aside from our master geologist. You can feel the connection to the past, can't you? Think of where these have been. And now they're yours."

The girls were enamored. But I'll be honest, I nearly leaned in and said, "Really? These are that old? That's amazing!" before catching myself. *It's part of the show, you idiot*, I told myself. *You're paying for the story.*

The three of us left that booth enchanted, to say the least.

Along the shoreline of Iceland, there's a crescent-shaped bay called Djúpalónssandur. The beach there is riddled with smooth, sea-polished stones. The signpost that greets you as you journey to the water calls these stones both "black lava pearls" and "elf rocks." There's no differentiating between the geological facts and the mythic wonders. Standing on that path, you can't help but think, *Is there some power in these stones? Are they really just the product of natural processes? Or did elves truly polish them? And why must those two options stand as opposites?* Perhaps both are true.

I'd never felt such a smooth stone before, not one that was just sitting out there in the open. Even the most polished of natural rocks along coastlines I'd visited still had some roughness to them, some imperfection. Not these; not the elf stones. My wife and I brought several of them home. Simple rocks, but they were pulsing with mystery.

"Elf stones," I told my girls, offering them in trembling hands. "They're magic."

The girls squealed in delight.

In the Catholic tradition, we love our medals and prayer cards and holy beads. I've kept a rosary in my pocket for years, though I rarely pray with it. I wear a golden cross around my neck, equal parts a symbol of my faith and a tribute to my grandparents who gave it to me as a gift for my Confirmation. There's something about the tangible presence of these simple objects, about the spiritual landscape to which they transport me. I draw comfort from simply adjusting that small cross or touching that old rosary—provided I can remember which pair of pants I've left it in.

These objects, made of earthly materials, serve as tactile reminders that we always stand upon the threshold between our world and the domain of the spiritual. Who's to say what power they hold? Who's to say what history they contain, what stories they point to?

The cross around my neck is more than its weight in gold because, to me, it also "holds" my grandmother and grandfather. I've touched that rosary in my pocket to holy sites around the world. More than that, I'm reminded of the countless pilgrims the world over who cling to the rosary in prayer, and to the holy women and men beyond my own faith tradition who also pray with beads, who hold sacred the mandala-shaped instrument of spiritual growth.

These simple objects *can* work miracles, of course. But their more mundane purpose is to remind us that we are part of a larger story. They position us squarely at the threshold of what we can see and what we can only imagine: the lava rock and the elf stone; the Renaissance Faire trinket that dares us to dream and wonder and hope.

AND NOW, CROSS THE THRESHOLD THAT LINKS THE ORDINARY TO THE FANTASTICAL.

As you walk away, you can't shake the feeling that you've been cheated somehow. That no matter how low a price you may have haggled for, the stones currently in your pocket are worth far less. There's no magic, you say to yourself. They're just stones. And I'm a fool. Unless . . .

You pause. You lean against the old wall of the town square. You draw the leather pouch from your pocket and the stones from the pouch. You study them closely: their smoothness, their color, their glow. There is something about them. Something that makes you wonder: Are they magical? Whose were they? Where did they come from? And why did they catch your attention in the first place? Your thoughts are lifted; your imagination freed to roam. They could be just stones, or they could be something more. Perhaps you'll find out as you continue to make your way. The possibility makes you smile.

The magic stones exude mystery.
How is it that such ordinary objects can conjure in our minds the extraordinary?

THE FIFTH CONTEMPLATION

The Familiar, or, Embracing the Spirit Guide

STEP INTO ADVENTURE.

You pause to look out over the horizon. The rolling hills sweep gently downward, a cascade of unfolding grass and green. The path ahead is clear, your walking stick is clasped firmly in your hand, and your bootlaces are tied and secure. Yet, you pause. You exhale slowly. You wonder where it is you're headed, and whether you have the wherewithal to get there.

"Into the unknown, eh?" a voice says from behind you.

You spin around, trying to find the source of the sudden sound. You raise your staff in a meager defense.

"Who's there?" you say.

"You've never been this far from home, right?" The voice is over your left shoulder now. You bat at it with an open palm, as though swatting at a bug. "You'll be tested."

"Show yourself," you say. You hope you sound strong, brave. You're pretty sure your voice cracked.

Then, just in front of you, a swirl of energy and wind appears, a mini cosmic tornado. You realize quite suddenly that you're staring at an animal. Well, a creature of some sort. It has horns and a furry snout and knowing eyes. It shimmers in the sun, and you can't tell if it's changing shape or if your eyes still need time to adjust to its sudden appearance. It floats just above the ground, but you're pretty sure if you reached out to touch it, your hand would pass right through.

"Hope you can handle it," the creature says.

"Who are you?" you stammer. "What are you?"

The creature shrugs, smiles. It spreads its arms wide, and you realize with just a touch of trepidation that its hands—paws?—are clawed. "I'm your spirit guide," the thing declares. "And I'm really looking forward to this little adventure we're on."

Turn to the ordinary.

The terms *familiar* and *spirit guide* can be used interchangeably. Regardless of the term you prefer, what we're talking about are spiritual companions of some power, often in the form of animals that offer both metaphysical guidance and practical support to their would-be master. These kinds of characters show up in fairy tales, legends, myths, and across the modern fantasy genre.

Often, a spirit guide can act as a go-between for a hero and the spirit world. The spirit guide might intercede at a key moment, offer an essential bit of wisdom, or simply encourage our hero when they're down.

The reason I like the term *familiar* is because of what it implies: This spirit guide isn't *random*; this spirit guide has done their homework. This spirit guide is familiar with me in all of my idiosyncrasies, needs, and desires. And this spirit guide is bound to me in an intimate way, tasked with bringing my story to some hope-filled conclusion. There's a companionship, too, that this term stirs in me, a sense of friendship (though that's certainly not always the case in literature). But I prefer this image of a companion spirit who is acting for my greater good, even when I'm not aware of it happening.

When I was young, I learned the guardian angel prayer: *Angel of God, my guardian dear, to whom God's love commits me here, ever this day be at my side, to light and guard, to rule and guide. Amen.*[28] The idea of a guardian angel may sound cute, especially since they're so often depicted as plump, little-winged children floating upon clouds above our own childish heads. This sing-songy prayer only reinforces the notion.

But let's sit with this idea of guardian angels for just a moment because of what it suggests: A specific angel—a being of spiritual power and mystery—has been assigned to guide each of us, tasked with offering us light and wisdom as we discern our unique vocational path. What does this tell us about God? We're reminded again that God takes a personal, intimate interest in our unfolding stories. So much so that God has paired us with a unique spiritual guide so that we don't have to make the journey alone.

The truth that our accompanying angels point to is that the spiritual realm is much nearer than we think, that just beyond our vision is a plane of otherworldly wonders and powers and delights. And we're invited in. We're invited to walk that road, straddling the spiritual and the temporal, in the company of a being uniquely companioned to us.

This is important. We often need spiritual help to navigate the temporal decisions before us. In the Ignatian tradition, we speak of discerning the spirits. We are constantly tasked with assessing the repercussions of decisions big and small. These decisions have a spiritual dimension. Are our choices leading us closer to God? Or are they instead serving—to borrow an Ignatian turn of phrase—the "enemy of our human nature?" Put another way, are we becoming more authentically ourselves through our decision making, or are we losing something inherent to our human nature?

These are spiritual questions. It's encouraging, then, to know we have a spiritual companion, a guide, one who is intimately *familiar* with our stories. Ignatius tells us to discern those spirits, to listen to the still, quiet voice of God and God's Spirit at work around us.

And now, cross the threshold linking the ordinary and fantastical.

"I don't understand," you say. "Why do I need a spirit guide? Why haven't you ever revealed yourself before? Why . . . " Your voice trails off.

The creature shrugs again. "Who's to say I haven't revealed myself before?"

"I think I'd remember seeing a . . . a . . ." You can't quite articulate what it is you see before you.

"Is it in the seeing that the revelation takes place?" the creature asks. "Or does the revelation happen somewhere more hidden?" The thing strokes what might be considered a beard. "I wonder. There are many at work in this world doing good things. And yet, you can't name them all. But still, good flows to you. Is that revelatory? Or is that companionship by another route?"

You shake your head. The thing is making no sense. "So, you're here to guide me. What am I supposed to do, then? Where am I supposed to go?"

"You're already on the path," the creature says. "I don't think it's a guide you need." And then, as suddenly as the creature appeared, it vanishes.

The intimacy of a spirit guide reminds us that we are worth knowing at the deepest level—and that our story matters. But do we believe that ourselves?

THE SIXTH CONTEMPLATION

The Fairies, or, Paying Attention to the Magic All Around

Step into adventure.

As you walk along the smooth and level path, you begin to hum. The melody is one you know well, but the name of the song is lost somewhere in the recesses of your mind. No matter. The tune is happy and so are you. You're moving along quickly, one confident stride after another. The terrain is pleasant: Short prickly shrubs and the occasional stunted tree frame your path. You're walking along a ridgeline; you can see for miles and miles in all directions. The sun is high and the clouds are sparse and the firmness of the ground beneath your feet gives you a giddy sort of confidence.

You can do this.

The tiny pinpricks of light dancing all around you seem to agree. They bounce on the breeze like balloons in a wind tunnel, flickering like a host of tiny candles. These little lights have a heaviness to them, a misty quality, and it encompasses you like a grandmother's hug.

That's when you realize you're not alone.

You slow your pace, glancing to your left and then to your right. You strain to hear the broken twig of a misplaced foot, the stifled cough of a tickled throat, or even a loud, "Hey, you there, stop!"

But there's nothing.

"I could sure use that spirit guide about now," you mutter under your breath.

And that's when a gentle voice whispers from somewhere just up ahead: "What need is there for a guide when you have arrived where you are going?"

Your feet freeze in place. You squint into the near distance, through the blinking lights and the sudden, rolling mist at what you can only assume is a cadre of tiny, winged people bouncing in and out of existence.

"You have come to the land of the Ridgeline Fairies. And you are very welcome here." The voice, you decide, is coming from just up ahead, from a small and beautiful woman with wings that glisten like dew in the morning sun. She wears a gown of golden leaves and a smile of joy and kindness. That is—when you can see her. Because like the other fairies hovering all around you, she seems to blink in and out of existence.

Suddenly she reappears, this time with a frown. You realize then that you've said nothing in response to her hospitality.

"Did you not intend to step into our realm?"

Turn to the ordinary.

My five-year-old daughter wonders if I believe in fairies. I have no evidence to disprove their existence. "The world is full of surprises," I say. "Hidden wonders." It's good enough.

We're looking for fairies along the wooded path near our house. We walk amid the tall, tall trees and along the quietly trickling stream and through the backyards of neighbors until we come to a place covered in stones. Big, ponderous boulders, arranged in a half circle, like campers around a campfire.

Here, she assures me, is where the fairies live.

On occasion, my daughter expresses her worry over the presence of dark fairies. She concocts potions with her friends. "Can't you make one to ward off dark magic?" I ask. It's a good question. She consults her contemporaries.

Indeed, such a potion is possible.

And still, we walk that wooded path. Since no fairies have been sighted yet, we make our way down toward the stream. Water bugs drift atop the water's surface. Leaves drift down and come to rest on plant roots and dirt. There's a serenity here, too, drifting. We let it encircle and enfold us with the sounds of birdsong and the chittering of squirrels and the soft noises of other things speaking to us in this tiny alcove of forest.

But we hear no fairies. We see no fairies. We say nothing.

And then a sudden snapping sound, the splitting of wooden branches held high above. There is no drifting now: The branch, a big old thing, crashes down abruptly, loudly, unceremoniously.

It lands at my feet.

"That was close," I say.

"Fairies?"

"Mmm," I say, and shrug. "It's a nice walking stick, though."

My daughter nods, reaches for it. Hefts it in her hand. Then she hands it back. "I'll sand it down for you," I say.

She continues playing in the stream, assessing the bugs, chasing after fairies. We see none.

I hold that branch in my hand, surprised how smooth it already is. I pull at the loose bark, dust off the edges, wonder at the tiny markings along its length.

When we get home, I pull out a knife and some sandpaper. It's a quick job. I hand it to my daughter.

"From the fairies," I say. She nods.

The next day she paints the staff: a collision of color and texture.

"Close call on that falling branch," I say to my wife. "That would've left a mark."

"Dark fairies," she says with a shrug. "Or maybe light."

"Light, I hope," I say.

Perhaps we do believe in fairies.

There are days when my daughters ask me directly: "Daddy, do you believe in fairies?" I always respond, "Do you?" There's another variation of that question: "Are there really fairies, Daddy?" My answer to that one is, "What do you think?" I know I'm playing with fire. But answer me this: Have *you* seen proof that fairies *don't* exist?

When it comes to the spiritual life, I'm less concerned with compiling an accurate encyclopedia of supernatural critters and more concerned with developing a disposition that is mindful of and reverent toward them, toward all of God's enchanted creation. When we say that *God is in all things* and that *All things conspire together for God's greater glory and the good of all people*, we do so never having a full picture of all that is entailed.

It's not a matter of *knowing* how this particular "thing" in front of me holds the holy potential of God's great goodness; it's more about *trusting* that God is at work everywhere—even here. The veil between our world and the spiritual is so thin as to be an open door. Do we simply need to clean our glasses so that we can see more clearly the spiritual gleam upon our temporal affairs?

God is in all things. What are those things? That irritating neighbor and that clogged sink and that missed flight and that devastating bit of news. We may not call all these things "good," but we do call them opportunities to once again encounter the living God who is simultaneously vast and beyond and yet also intimate and nearby.

This disposition is not one easily sustained. Sure, we find God in the birth of a newborn, a promotion at work, or a particularly inspiring passage from a holy text. Perhaps we even seek God out in such places. But it's also true that it's not a hard task to name those places and people, those headlines and hardships, that seem devoid of any divine spark.

We must trust that God is here, too.

That's why I tell my girls that, for me, the jury is out on fairies. Not because I expect to trip over one in the supermarket but because I have to believe that the world is so much larger than we know. I see the world as pulsing with graces and surprises and the presence of a God beyond our knowing.

We step into this world each and every moment. In this world, we witness miracles each and every day; some of them break our hearts. We glimpse the impossible—or, what to us seems impossible. And we muddle onward.

Let us not grow numb to the twinkling lights that surround us.

And now, cross the threshold that links the ordinary to the fantastical.

"No," you stammer, "I didn't mean to come here. I don't think I did, at least."

There's a chittering noise from the light and the fog and then, "How can you not know where you already are? And how can you arrive where you do not intend?"

You shake your head, smacking your lips in frustration. "I'm just passing through," you say. "I mean you no harm."

That chittering sound again. It sounds like laughter. "It is not harm we see in you," the voice says.

You wait for the voice to say more, but silence fills the space, as palpable as the fog and as distracting as the lights. Finally, you say, "I'm simply passing through."

"But that is impossible," the lead fairy says. "How can you pass through all that is?"

And to that, you have no response. So you simply bow your head and keep walking.

Fairies exist to remind us that the universe is greater than we can possibly imagine. But do we readily seek out such enchantment?

THE SEVENTH CONTEMPLATION

The Pixies, or, Remembering the Mischief of the World

STEP INTO ADVENTURE.

The air assumes a sharp briskness as you continue walking. You pull your cloak tighter. You tuck your chin into your chest. You keep your gaze low and your eyes on the misty path at your feet. You try to rekindle just a spark's worth of the confidence you previously felt.

You ignore the twinkling lights and the deepening fog and the alarm in the tiny voices dancing all around you.

And then, one voice cuts sharper than the rest. "You've brought the offering, then?"

You pause, one foot held in midair, dangling just above the mud and grass. Your curiosity is piqued. "The offering?"

"Aye, yes, they'll never let you proceed without it."

The other voices have dimmed. All you can hear is this one, this singular pointed voice.

"I—I don't know what you mean. Who needs an offering? And what—"

"Ah—he didn't tell you then. Typical."

"Who didn't tell me?"

"The wizard. Always disrupting honest folks' lives and leading them out here without a feathertip's worth of preparation."

You chew on those words. You dislike the aftertaste. "There have been others?"

Laughter. "You thought you were the only one? No, no. The wizard loves to lure unsuspecting folks into the wild."

"Lure?" You don't like that word, not at all.

"What would you call it?"

You have no response. So instead, you ask a question: "What do you mean about an offering?"

Laughter again. "Listen. Take my advice. You're not going to want to go any further without an offering."

You realize quite suddenly that the other voices have completely faded; all you can hear is this mysterious newcomer. And you realize, too, that whoever they are, they still haven't answered any of your questions.

But you know one thing for certain: You can barely remember what it felt like to feel confident in your decision. And, without even realizing it, you glance back the way you've come.

TURN TO THE ORDINARY.

Pixies are mischievous—that's the defining trait that sets them apart from the wider world of fairies. They sow a bit of chaos, a bit of trouble, a bit of discord, a bit of misdirection. If you're a scholar of folklore, perhaps you know this. Perhaps you have an even more articulate way of differentiating these fairy varieties. Perhaps you're rolling your eyes at my ham-fisted efforts.

But if you're not such a scholar, you might wonder why anyone would go through such trouble to differentiate these creatures in the first place. You might not have even realized there was a distinction regarding pixies worth articulating. You, too, might be rolling your eyes at my bumbling efforts to paint such a picture.

And herein lies the point: Fairies or pixies—who is to say? They sure seem like the same thing to our hasty human eyes. It's not worth our time or effort to know there's a difference, let alone to go about the work of differentiating them.

I wonder if that's not true in our spiritual lives. We often find ourselves assailed by so many voices, thoughts, ideas, and hidden whispers that disentangling them seems to be a fool's errand, and a wasteful one at that.

Ignatian spirituality is built on discernment, on "discerning the spirits" that dance about in our spiritual lives. Why? Because there *are* different spirits, different voices. Knowing which are good and which are unhelpful is essential to making good decisions—decisions that drive the daily actions of our lives. Too often, these spirits appear to be identical. They offer advice that sounds good, but how are we supposed to know which to listen to, which to act upon?

The word *mischief* is helpful. It shares a prefix with the word *misdirection.* This prefix implies something bad or badly considered. In many ways, the spiritual life is an ongoing exercise in trajectory-setting, in choosing a direction for our lives and consistently moving along that path. Misdirection doesn't necessarily mean we make a sudden U-turn. Misdirection may result from a minor miscalculation made on bad or insufficient data. But we might not realize we've miscalculated until we're quite far along the wrong path.

That's why we need to be attuned to those voices of mischief present in our lives. We need to carefully assess the direction they're encouraging and the trajectory they may set our lives upon. We need to look not simply at the next step but at the ultimate destination. In fact, we need clarity on where we hope to go. And then we need to decide if this voice is helping us get closer to that place, or if it is pushing us off course.

AND NOW, CROSS THE THRESHOLD THAT LINKS THE ORDINARY TO THE FANTASTICAL.

You stand there, frozen. There's an uncomfortable feeling in your gut as the mysterious voice continues to prance about between your ears.

"The wizard always does this," the voice insists. "Bringing ill-prepared travelers out and onto the road and then leaving them to their own devices. Quite inconsiderate, if you ask me."

The words feel true. They resonate at some level. But they sound discordant, incomplete. There's more here.

"No," you say slowly. "That can't be right."

You hear the verbal equivalent of a shrug. "I'd just hate to see you waste your time."

"Why do you care?"

The voice pauses, the answer hanging somewhere in that cold misty air. That's when you realize something: The words hurt because they imply that you're not special, that somehow your worth was defined by the assumption that the wizard had invited no others along this path. Hurt though they might make you feel, those words say nothing about the correctness of your journey or the path that you're on.

It's your pride that stings. But your pride has nothing to do with where you're going.

"You don't care," you say finally. "You're just trying to distract me."

That sound again—the shrug. "You still don't have an offering," the voice says undeterred. "I wouldn't want to go where you're going without one."

"I think I'll take my chances," you say. And as you do, the din of other tiny voices returns, growing stronger even as the mischievous one begins to fade. You're surrounded by lights once more and the mist feels just a touch less ominous.

You decide to keep walking.

A pixie arrives to cause mischief and misdirection. Can we hold firm to our purpose even when mischievous voices ring in our ears?

THE EIGHTH CONTEMPLATION

The Forest, or That Place Where We Get Knocked Around

STEP INTO ADVENTURE.

The forest holds secrets—this, you know. This, you expect. What else would a winding road through misty darkness hold? You signed up for adventure, and here it is. You knew the forest would be here, that you'd arrive at this moment, this place. Still, you feel unprepared, unwelcome, and unwell.

Ancient trees stoop low to cast their shadows upon your chosen path. Winding roots and wayward branches erupt into view and then vanish back into the earth and air. Those same trees soar high above you, too. They form a canopy that blots out the sun. The light that remains to guide you is cold and eerie. You push aside dangling vines, keeping your eyes set on your feet on the path. You can do this.

There are sounds all around you—squeaks and squawks and the rustle of tiny feet and occasionally something larger. You draw some dark comfort from knowing that the forest is alive, that you are not the only one passing through. Still—you move quickly, not daring to pause to look closely at your fellow voyagers. You fear the sight of teeth and yellow eyes and mangled claws.

One foot in front of the other. You can't go over it; you can't go under it; you must go through it. And so you do, wishing all the while the wizard had provided a shortcut, or your spirit guide would pipe up with a cheat code, or those so-called magic stones in your pocket might do something useful. There's no getting around it, literally. You try to push from your mind the stories you've heard and the legends you've learned and the warnings of so many who have unwisely found themselves traipsing through this same wooded ground.

And though you keep putting one foot in front of the other, determined to reach your destination, whatever it might be, you can't shake the feeling that something is about to happen. Some hole in the ground will open wide and gobble you up. Some monster will descend from the leafy canopy and rip your limbs clear off your body. Some poisoned mushroom will prick your skin and draw the blood straight out of your veins.

The forest holds its secrets—this, you know. But which secret is yours to unravel? Which secret holds some hidden truth into your future?

* * *

Turn to the ordinary.

My wife and I were young and comically ill-prepared the first time we went backpacking. We had never done such a thing before, neither of us, not individually and certainly not together. I'd barely ever been camping. All the same, we bought the gear, packed it up tight in our newly acquired backpacks and set off for the Great Smoky Mountains.

We had plotted our route, of course. That's a basic best practice. We'd left that info with our parents—though, after driving the seven hours from Indianapolis to our designated starting point in Tennessee, it seemed as if the best our parents might do with that info was use it to find our long-decayed bodies.

We arrived for our four-day journey, parked our car, and pulled out our gear. We marched right on up to the trailhead, studying the welcome information with a near academic rigor.

"Aggressive bear activity," I read aloud. "That doesn't sound great."

"Looks like we won't be taking that route," my wife said. We quickly made some adjustments to our map, called our parents, and reexamined our path.

"All good," we declared, and into the forest we plunged.

We didn't see any bears along our path. And when we came to a roaring river, we also didn't see a bridge.

"I don't think we should wade through, right?" I asked.

"Definitely not," my not-at-all-tall wife replied. "At best we get soaked; at worst, we get washed away."

"That's a fair point."

We turned back, opting to stay dry.

That was two strikes, though how many were allotted and which metaphoric game we were playing, we couldn't quite say. But the days were beautiful, filled with majestic views, quiet paths, and good conversation between two young people in the early stages of their relationship.

The nights were peaceful, too. We had encountered very few fellow travelers along our route, and so one night when we heard voices coming along the path up to our campsite, we found ourselves eager to share some company. We had games to play and stories to tell and we wondered how these other folks had navigated the missing bridge. The sun was low and the next campsite far.

And yet . . .

No one appeared.

We waited and watched and worried. We *had* heard voices, right? Had they turned back? That seemed unlikely because we were too far from another site. But neither had anyone passed by. And certainly no one was here with us.

Three strikes: Aggressive bears, a missing bridge, and ghosts.

We've not been backpacking since.

A friend of mine once remarked that when God leads the Israelites out of Egypt, it's worth remembering that—though they are freed—they are immediately plunged into the wilderness. They are liberated from oppression and slavery and set loose in an unforgiving, untamed land. The status quo has been shattered (which was a good thing), but a new and unexpected journey immediately begins (and the way ahead was perilous).

The Israelites face many choices, many crossroads, and many hinge moments, and they frequently fall short. God is both their companion and their destination—the best of travel buddies and the best of maps. Yet the road is still challenging and uncertain. Liberation from the status quo does not mean an easy or quick path to the next best thing. It means work and discernment and a slow, steady muddling onward. Even when you're headed for the Promised Land, the promises often take unexpected and unwanted turns.

Do we persevere despite it all? We can go back, surrender to the old ways and the decaying status quo, and give up on the adventure. Or we can keep going. We can respond as best we can to the shocks and surprises. We can find a new route that accounts for downed bridges and campsites overrun with aggressive bears because we knew the forest would test us. That's its role in the story. The forest is full of challenge, but it's full of wonder, too. We marvel not only at the mysteries hidden in the forest but also at the mysteries that are revealed in ourselves. We marvel at how we rise to the occasion because what we learn in the forest just might come in handy somewhere a bit further down the road.

* * *

AND NOW, CROSS THE THRESHOLD THAT LINKS THE ORDINARY TO THE FANTASTICAL.

You rub your jaw, studying the downed tree in front of you. It's a perfect excuse to turn back. The road is blocked; how are you expected to pass? You've given it your all. Why not throw in the towel now? What more can really be expected of you?

Still. Your eyes examine that fallen tree, running over its decaying bark. You spy a weak point. One good kick with the business end of your boot should do the trick. But if you do it, if you push on, there's no turning back. You'll have kicked in your last excuse—or so you tell yourself.

Something in the back of your mind whispers a word of encouragement. Something in the back of your mind beckons you onward. Something in the back of your mind wants you to see more of what this forest has to offer.

You're curious, you realize. You've read enough about this place to know there's more to see. That curiosity breathes a warmth into your body, or is that the stones in your pocket?

Either way, you break through that fallen tree and press on.

The forest is full of unexpected challenges. But if we expect the inevitable obstacles, when they appear, do we transform them into opportunities?

THE NINTH CONTEMPLATION

The Genius Loci, or, What We Owe the Place

Step into adventure.

They say there's a place on the far side of the forest where creatures of legend roam free. The rain that falls there is gentle, kissing the deep roots of old, old trees that climb high toward the sun. They say there is always a slight breeze, enough to ruffle your hair and caress your face and call forth a smile from your weary lips.

That smile, they say, never fades thereafter. Some claim the winds that blow in that place follow you home, dancing about your feet, tugging at your hair and your collar and your heart. It tickles, they say, like joy brushing up against your neck, bashful. How can you keep from smiling?

That's what they say, at least. And they say it's still there, waiting, that clearing deep, deep in the forest. The creatures—all fur and wings and magical horns—still roam, and the trees still reach for those few clouds in the sky.

But no one makes the journey. Not anymore. It's so far into the forest, after all, and the trees are high and full and the path is long and winding. And the rain here on the near side of the forest may be hard and unpredictable but the plants still grow. Why bother? Who has the time? Leave the old creatures in peace.

But you have a different theory. Because they say something else, too. They say that deep, deep in the forest, in that clearing of peace and beauty and wonder is a vineyard: rows and rows of perfect vines, meticulously manicured, grapes nestled within, ready to be plucked.

And they say it's still that way: perfect, meticulous, well-kept.

Who's doing the keeping? That's what you say, what you wonder.

And you have another theory: Maybe we're all just a little afraid to meet the keeper of that perfect place, the master of the creatures of legend, the one who exhales that breath of joyful air.

Perhaps we're better off here, and perfection is better left over there on the far side of the forest.

"Not so," comes a voice in your ear. Your spirit guide has returned. "Not so at all. Onward!"

You feel the warmth of the magic stones glowing in your pocket; you marvel at the runes lit up along your staff. And you decide to continue on in search of you-know-not-what. Something calls to you from the forest's depths. Someone. Somewhere.

A place of power and poignancy and potential. Perhaps this is the reason you are here.

TURN TO THE ORDINARY.

Genius loci translates from Latin to "the spirit of the place."

We might imagine some creature of Faerie—a powerful essence personified and bound to a given location—prowling about an old castle or floating lovingly above a pristine pond. In our imagination, we see winged beings, or angry demons, or gentle old pilgrims appearing without warning to bestow either a gift or a curse, and then vanishing into the mist just as suddenly as they arrived.

When this happens, we know we've entered a specific place that is the domain of another who wields a power beyond what we are familiar with. Perhaps we've come here intentionally; perhaps we've stumbled in accidentally. Either way, we know that something else—actually, some*one* else—is here with us now, and they have a thing or two to share.

In some ways, this is the goal of a pilgrimage. We journey to holy places—temples and churches and shrines—not only to observe the architecture and experience the sights and sounds, but also to walk in the footsteps of other people. We bask in their legacy so that we can learn from their example. We grapple with the path they themselves set out upon to help guide us in reaching our own destinations.

Recall that in the Catholic tradition, we look to and are part of the communion of saints, which includes all people who have wrestled with what it means to live a life of holiness. These ancestors have pulled at the thread of spirituality, grasping for its meaning, and have consequently provided us with examples of faith in action. But these are not merely stories of the past. The holy women and men who paved our way are still with us, still in our company, always here to guide us, pray for us, celebrate with us. After all, don't we profess belief in the Resurrection of the Dead and the life of the world to come?

When we visit these holy places, we aren't simply spiritual tourists; we are spiritual seekers. And we seek not only a place but also a people. What might we learn from those who stood on this same holy ground?

I cheated when I made my pilgrimage to the Ignatian places. I took a bus, which is much faster than walking and a lot easier on the feet. All the same, I ventured to those key locales in the life story of St. Ignatius of Loyola. I stood in the room where he was born. I drove past the town where he was wounded, famously struck by a French cannonball and sent from the battlefield back to his home to heal. I prayed before the image of Our Lady of Montserrat, the very one in front of which he laid down his sword as the symbol of his old life, now forsaken, and committed himself to God. I attended Mass in the chapel built into the rocky outcropping in Manresa, the sacred space where Ignatius penned his collection of meditations and exercises for retreatants we know as the Spiritual Exercises.

I went to all these places. I studied the ancient stones and the soaring ceilings and the winding pathways and the inspired art. I prayed in community, and I took time to be by myself. I knew the story of Ignatius and his gradual conversion from a worldly knight to a mystic saint by heart, and putting my own body in the very real places in which this conversion had occurred was deeply consoling.

But it wasn't only a reflective experience, nor was it an academic one. There was something powerful about grounding myself in these Ignatian places. Ignatius of Loyola was *here*. But not just in the past. Ignatius remains in these places now, in the present. Those who cross the threshold of these Ignatian places do so seeking to learn something new about life from Ignatius today: not a history lesson but a way to make meaning now. Ignatius's spirit reverberates in each and every hallway. His words, his mission, his hopes, and his failures. I imagine every person who walks along the Ignatian way is doing so to glimpse something of the saint, to see not just what Ignatius *did* but how Ignatius's life might speak to the contemporary pilgrim in the present.

How did the Spirit manifest in Ignatius? What is the life of Ignatius of Loyola saying *to me*? How does that same Spirit's manifestation in Ignatius speak to and move me here, in my everyday life back in the United States?

We can pray about these things from the comfort of our home, of course. But there's something potent about standing in the place, gazing up at the same walls and breathing the same air as we dare to reach across the threshold of time and clasp hands with another pilgrim from another era. The physical and the spiritual are woven together in the very being of our bodies, which then carry us onward.

This is the heart of pilgrimage.

AND NOW, CROSS THE THRESHOLD THAT LINKS THE ORDINARY TO THE FANTASTICAL.

You can't be sure how far you are from the center of the forest, from the mystical call you feel in your bones. It's energizing. You want to respond. You know you're headed in the right direction.

And yet, with every step you take, you realize that there are stories all around you. Rushing to the end, rushing to that sacred space, might cause you to miss something just as sacred right here at your feet.

You wonder where this sudden realization has come from. You wonder if the forest's misty air is beginning to get to you. But you also smile because you know you're on the right path.

And more important, you've brought the right disposition.

"Onward," the voice whispers again in your ear. "But don't get tripped up looking only at your feet."

**The genius loci whispers to us from the holy ground upon which we stand—
and from the holy ground to which we go.
What are we called to notice?**

THE TENTH CONTEMPLATION

The Centaur, or, Beyond Our Usual Expectations

STEP INTO ADVENTURE.

A new sound joins the forest choir: the clip-clop-clip-clop of hooves. You slow your own pace, try to decipher the direction from which the horse is walking. Are you on a collision course? Have you already been seen? A bolt of anxiety pulses through your body as you settle into the unease.

You don't recall any nearby castles on any maps you've seen of the forest. You feel relatively confident you're not about to be apprehended by a patrol of angry soldiers. And it seems to you that you're much too deep in this forest to be ambushed by robbers or thieves—this is not a common enough path to justify such an operation.

So, who have you stumbled upon? Another of the wizard's wandering pilgrims? Or someone else?

Clip-clop, clip-clop. Clip. Clop.

You realize suddenly that the horse's pace has slowed to match yours. You feel exposed, even standing ankle deep in thick grass and surrounded by towering trees. But still, you press on, slowly, listening. You feel strange eyes on you, but you keep yours straight ahead.

"Been quite some time since I've seen a human in these parts."

The voice is booming, merry, and directly to your left. You spin, raising your staff and meeting the eyes of a bald and bearded man. He smiles, a chuckle bouncing out of his mouth. He looms tall above you—your head comes up to his waist—but what else would you expect when met by someone on horseback?

Clip-clop, clip-clop.

But something isn't right. Did he say you were a human as though he was not?

"I'm glad for the company," you say. "And I'm impressed your horse doesn't need to stay on the path."

"Oh-ho!" the man bellows. "My horse indeed!" And with a leap and bound, the Centaur lands right in front of you: towering, majestic, wild and fierce. "Haven't seen one of my kind before, I think. This sort of horse doesn't need a path. These wilds are ours, but you're welcome to pass through." Another booming laugh. "But if you're to survive out here, you might give a little less credence to what you think you see and hear, and a lot more to what's standing right in front of you."

* * *

Turn to the Ordinary.

Centaurs come from Greek mythology. Half-horse and half-human, they're often depicted as barbaric, savage, and drunk. They're stereotyped as lustful. One origin story attributes the birth of all centaurs to an unfortunate collision of lust, trickery, and anger. But none of that need concern us here.

I am more enchanted by the *idea* of a centaur—or any such being that melds multiple creatures into one. A faun, a griffin, a jackelope, and so on. Who was the first person to imagine such a thing? Who first allowed their creativity to run wild, ignoring the obvious so as to embrace the spectacular?

I can only assume that a person from eons ago was walking in the woods or standing in the fields and looked up to see a horse and its rider upon the horizon. Instead of drawing a logical conclusion that they were seeing some guy or gal on a horse, this individual saw in that distant figure something entirely new.

Was that person frightened? Did they run, screaming, into the village? "A horse-man hybrid is on the way! Run for your lives!" Did somebody else poke their head out of a shop doorway and make the dry observation, "Horse-man hybrid is a mouthful; let's just call it a 'centaur'" before fleeing for their lives? Or did that villager allow the idea of the centaur to enchant their imagination and lead them to wonder what other mysterious beings exist in this wide world?

We have two options when greeted with the unknown. The first is to allow fear to compel us into hiding, and we shrink our own imagination. The second is to embrace curiosity, which propels us out of ourselves and our ordinary status quo.

There is a third option, I suppose, and it's likely the one we turn to most readily. It's the option that rationalizes away and places in a box of preconceived notions the mystery that we see. This is the reaction that reduces the unknown to knowable, more easily believable, parts. This isn't always a bad thing, to be sure. It's how we make advancements in our own base of knowledge, our societal understanding of reality. But it can be limiting. Disenchanting. Small.

What happens when we take a similar approach to the spiritual life? I believe God is often trying to blow up our preconceived notions of who God is and how God is calling us into the world. When presented in prayer with the proverbial centaur, we are quick to say, "No, no. That can only be a human on a horse. Nothing more; nothing to see here. Same old, same old. And now I can continue about my day."

What if, instead, our disposition in prayer always makes room for the totally unexpected, the new and the strange and the spectacular? What if we *expect* a centaur every time we hear the clip-clop of hooves? How would the trajectory of our spiritual lives change?

* * *

And now, cross the threshold that links the ordinary to the fantastical.

The Centaur cannot keep his hooves still. He constantly lifts one, drops another, creating an ongoing cloud of dust. You wonder if that dust helps him hide his true form. You wonder if that dust is clouding your own perception of things.

"The funny thing is," the Centaur says, "I see humans all the time. But never here, never this far in."

"How?" you ask. "I mean, I would have thought I'd have heard about it."

"No one hears about it," the Centaur laughs. "No one really sees what they don't expect to find. A centaur among the common horses! Impossible." The laughter continues.

"But if no one even sees you, or pays attention to you, I guess, then why bother? Why waste your time with horses and humans?"

The Centaur nods to himself, pulls at the leaves tangled in his beard. "Can't hurt to try, right? Humans are interesting. You never know when one might actually see what's standing right in front of them! Ha!"

But you wonder: If creatures of lore and legend as big as a centaur have been walking among your people, what else is there, watching? Have they been there the whole time? And what do you need to do to truly see?

The centaur leaps from the deep forest to remind us that we have more to see. But do we trust our imagination to lead us along a path of impossibilities?

THE ELEVENTH CONTEMPLATION

The Elves, or, The Perfection We Seek

STEP INTO ADVENTURE.

They appear suddenly out of the mist and foliage, all golden hoods and swinging medallions, and chanting. It begins as a hum, a vibration you feel in your very bones, but soon the resonant punctuation of words unfolds. You don't know the language, of course, but the meaning of this ancient tongue flows through you. You find yourself enchanted—quite literally. You stand still, rocking in your boots, feeling a warmth and peace envelope you.

And then—you're surrounded.

But you have no fear, no worry. Just a dull sense of longing, an ache in your bones as you stare at these beautiful creatures, these elves. A sad smile crosses your face, and you spread your arms wide.

"I'm here," you say. "Take me in."

But the elves say nothing in response. They simply continue their chanting, swing their medallions left and right, left and right. With each swing, you realize, a new wave of peace passes through you. With each swing, you realize, a new green shoot bursts through the forest floor. With each swing, you realize, you glimpse something new of what the world could be—of what you could be in it.

There are nine elves now, each standing just beyond arm's reach. Swinging, swaying, chanting, humming. It's beautiful, majestic. There's nothing more you could want.

But then—"Come along, friend," one elf says. "You cannot stay, but you may rest and wonder."

Wonder? Was that the right word? Surely, the elf meant "wander." Why would you want to wonder in this place? Surely, though, you'll want to explore.

You fall in line as the procession of elves departs from the quiet clearing. You realize you're excited. Nervous, even. What are you about to see? You suddenly feel quite inadequate, quite small. You try to steal a glance at your would-be hosts. You marvel at their golden robes, the aura of peace and beauty that surrounds them. And then—

And then you turn a corner and find yourself in a wooded oasis, a village of carefully crafted homes and sparkling sunlight.

"It's perfect," you gasp. And that's when you know that the elf was right: You cannot stay here.

Turn to the ordinary.

There is a line in the Gospel of Matthew: "Be perfect, just as your heavenly Father is perfect."[29] It's an anxiety-inducing line, particularly when read out of context. So much of disordered religious practice expects us to be perfect. We are tempted to hold ourselves up and compare our lives to others, to dwell on our shortcomings while idolizing those we presume have none. *I've failed here, but you've failed there. I'm better here, though I've not yet caught up to you there. I'll get there, though; I won't give up.*

We think God expects us to be perfect, but what does *perfect* mean? When compared to God, every human assumption of perfection necessarily falls short. And so, instead, we compare ourselves to those around us: to the big boss, the prom queen, the rich neighbor, the successful entrepreneur, the stunning model. We look at ourselves, our lives, and wonder why we are so inferior. Why do we fail so frequently? We dread falling behind; we tremble before the judgment of our parents, teachers, guests, spouses.

There's a delightful line in one of the songs from the Disney film *Moana 2*. Loto the boat builder says, "Perfection is a myth. . . . There's really only failing, then learning, then death." She's responding to the title of the song—"What Could Be Better Than This?"—and the insistence from her traveling companions that they've achieved a certain level of perfection. In other words, what could be better than sailing on the ocean?

Of course, if you don't care for sailing or the ocean, your response might be, "Just about anything." Which is, of course, the point. Perfection is in the eye of the beholder. Perfection is understood through the lens of your past experiences, future desires, dreams, hopes, and fears.

Perfection is also slippery. Exactly when you think you might have arrived, you find yourself not so sure. That perfect job you once had—did you not eventually look for a new challenge? How about that perfect vacation—did you not try to surpass it the following year? Perfection is a moving target.

So then, do we let the desire for perfection draw us out of ourselves into the vastness of the world? Or do we allow the idea of perfection to curdle within us? Do we permit the unrealized goal of perfection to shame us and cause crippling self-doubt to become lodged inside? We can be enchanted and delighted by what appears perfect in the moment or we can allow it to drive us mad.

Here's an important detail about that line of Scripture with which we began: It concludes the section of Matthew's Gospel in which Jesus encourages us to love our *enemies*. The perfection of God of which Jesus speaks is not an idol to worship; it's an action to embody. Perfection to Jesus, who is reflecting God's own self, is an outward, insistent movement of love that finds expression in an all-inclusive invitation that knows no restrictions.

Perhaps perfection is not a yearning after something we see and think we can never be. Perhaps perfection is a realization that all of us—everything we've got—are needed to complete God's dream. Perfection isn't a place where we arrive; it's the ongoing action of self-gift. In the giving, we all become more than we can yet imagine.

And now, cross the threshold that links the ordinary to the fantastical.

"You misunderstand," the elf says. "You do belong here. And you are very welcome."

You hadn't said anything since setting eyes upon the elven village. You wonder now if elves can read minds.

Beautiful, mind-reading creatures, you think.

"You cannot stay here because you cannot become all you must be," the elf continues. "What you can find here, my friend, is refreshment. Rejoice and be glad in this place, for we rejoice and are glad to have you among us. But then take that delight and go forth."

You shake your head. "What about me being here makes you glad? I'm just a . . ." You trail off. You feel your shoulders sink.

"Exactly," the old elf says. "You are just—" The elf waves a hand to encompass the ground upon which you stand. "And that is just right for now." A smile. "Come. Share in our joy and gladness. That is why we are, no?"

You puzzle over this final comment. And you realize, perhaps this really is a place to wonder. Curiosity, after all, is a powerful antidote to doubt.

**Elves reflect a beauty we desire.
Rather than judge ourselves as less-than
or as imperfect, can we instead offer who we are,
what we have, and learn along the way?**

THE TWELFTH CONTEMPLATION

The Feast, or, The Place Where All Are Welcome

STEP INTO ADVENTURE.

You've never seen such a long table. Made of polished oak, it's smooth and fragrant. The edges were left rough and natural, and the table is so big, it stretches out beyond your ability to see the far end. What's interesting is this table is just one of a dozen tables that have been set up for the great feast. You can't even guess at the number of seats lining these many tables.

The feast is outside, of course—you couldn't imagine a hall big enough to entertain so many guests. The food appears from the forest itself, each guest arriving with a tray of sparkling berries or freshly found nuts or cakes that smell of dreams. The elves are there, too, showing newcomers to their places, clasping hands and exchanging hugs and balancing their own plates of delights.

"Is this all for me?" you ask. The words fall out of your mouth before you can catch them, and you immediately blush.

The old elf next to you laughs. "For you? Perhaps. I suppose it all depends on your point of view. There's a place for you—just there, I believe—and there's food we hope you'll like. We're quite glad you're here to enjoy our hospitality but . . ."

You quickly step in, try to smooth over your arrogant question. "This was already planned. Of course."

The elf bows slightly. "Every first day of the new week, yes. All are welcome in this place."

You grin. "I can see that."

In addition to the elves, you spy a handful of centaurs and more than a few rabbits. There are deer and bears and squirrels and hawks. There are little blinking lights—the fairies, you presume—and a band of stout fellows with long, twirling beards. There are more, too: So many people and creatures, beings of all sorts, you can't begin to name them all. But they're here, all of them, together and at peace, delighting in one another's company.

"It's amazing," you whisper. "All these people."

"Amazing?" the elf asks with a chuckle. "Yes. I suppose it is."

TURN TO THE ORDINARY.

My friend and Jesuit priest Brian Christopher, who lives and works in Belize, once told me a story about a man who suffered from chronic alcoholism. On those occasions when the man dropped by the church rectory, Brian would share food and water and conversation. Over the years, they developed a sort of friendship. But the man would never come into the church itself.

One day, Brian found this man sitting outside the church, crying. "I just feel so bad that I can't go in. I want to go in. I want to receive Jesus." Brian asked, "Well, why *don't* you come in?"

"There was once a priest who told me that I'm not allowed," the man replied. "He told me that if I've been drinking, I can't come into church and receive Jesus."

Brian described the sadness he felt, and the sadness the man felt. "And I think even Jesus felt sad," Brian said. "I mean, here was a guy who was hungry for Jesus, and whatever pain he was carrying, he was trying to fill it up with alcohol. And he was killing himself. And he knew he was killing himself. And as a church, somebody said, 'No, no, you don't belong here.' That's not a church I want to be a part of. That's not a church that I *can be* a part of. If the church doesn't open for everybody, we shouldn't open our doors at all."

Pope Francis said something similar at World Youth Day 2023 in Lisbon, Portugal. Who is welcome in the church? "*Todos. Todos. Todos.*"

Everyone. Everyone. Everyone.

In the Catholic tradition, we say the source and summit of our faith is the Eucharist. I believe that the Eucharist is Jesus Christ who desires to enter deeply into our very selves. God isn't simply *out there*; God is here, now. We touch and taste God; we are sustained in a quite literal way by Christ.

We've put a lot of barriers around receiving the Eucharist. It makes sense, of course, that we educate and inform ourselves about what the Eucharist is, what Christ made present in our very midst means for you and for me. My daughters, for example, will need to complete their First Holy Communion studies before they receive the Eucharist. They are eager to do so.

But this speaks to a sense of understanding the truth of God present in the Eucharist. What are we really saying? We're saying that we are vessels of God, that God enters into our bodies not only to bless them but also to urge us onward as we build up God's great dream for the world. This is exciting and inclusive work. Our hope is that all people participate in God's dream, and that each of us becomes our fullest self.

We all want to sink into and live out our unique vocations, and to do so in community. We want to be anchored in and nourished by God's own self—a constant reminder that God is very near indeed and very active in our lives.

The Eucharist is meant to be a feast. Everyone is meant to be welcome. But too often, we throw up obstacles. We get in one another's way. We get in our *own* way. But God desires to draw near all the same. Nothing prevents God from entering our lives.

Unfortunately, we can turn a blind eye to that same God. We can work against the Christ who calls us to be members of the same mystical body. We can ignore the needs and the hopes and the struggles of people who share in this inherent identity.

I'm tempted, when picturing a great feast in a story, to assume we've reached the story's end. "Ah—the feast! Victory is at hand, and now we celebrate and bask in our glory!" But in fact this is not usually the case. The feast isn't the destination; it's one plot point along the way. Sometimes the gathering around the table ends poorly (as in the Red Wedding in *Game of Thrones*, for example); other times it is a healing event that brings people together.

The source and summit of the Catholic faith—the Eucharistic Feast—is meant to be bread for the journey. It's not meant to be a secret enclave where only a few gather; it's not the inner sanctum of a castle under siege. It's God's holy food for God's holy people, and it's meant to sustain us as we go about doing God's holy work.

We're all hungry. We all need to be fed. And we all need one another. That's why when we pray the Our Father we ask specifically for our daily bread. And we do so together.

And now, cross the threshold that links the ordinary to the fantastical.

"This is how it was meant to be, I think," the old elf continues. "A constant, open invitation to come as you are, as you're able, to be fed and then sent back."

"It's a lot of work," you say. "I mean, how do you organize such a thing? How do you ensure everyone gets what they need?"

The old elf turns, places a weathered hand on your shoulder. "You trust. And you give thanks. Trust and gratitude and delight—these three, they work miracles."

The feast is but one moment along the winding path of our story, but it is a moment of communal delight.
What prevents us from fully participating?

THE THIRTEENTH CONTEMPLATION

The Bard, or, The One Who Reminds Us of Our Legacy

Step into adventure.

"A song!" a single voice cries out from the end of the great banquet table.

"A song!" All the gathered voices join in a rowdy, joyous cry. Steins filled with bubbling beverages clatter against one another, bang on the wood of the table. Cheers and chants and excitement.

It seems the chaotic chorus has summoned a diminutive woman. She leaps up onto the table, kicking aside an empty platter and pulling from the strap on her back a mandolin. She grins an elfish smile, though she's no elf. Her hair is red and short, and her ears have a slight point at their tips. She's garbed in woodland wear, as though she's stepped out from the leaves themselves.

"A song," she says. Her words are not rowdy or loud, but firm and confident. She spins around on her left foot, her right foot pressed firmly against her left thigh, her knee bent at an angle. There are hundreds of beings gathered there eager to watch what's about to unfold, all eyes on the little mandolin player. You can't figure out how, but she's able to meet the gaze of everybody there.

And now, just for a second, she's locked eyes with you. Your heart flutters. Then, the bard closes her eyes and begins to pluck at the strings.

The song begins, low and lilting:

"From stars on high the dust does fall,
Upon our fields, e'er weeping.
One touch of grace does spring the bud,
Of season's change and kneading."

All eyes are on the bard now. The entire forest has fallen silent. You feel the enchantment wrap around your heart, your very soul. You feel it seep in and draw out something from within. You feel warmth.

"And now, a song for our guest," the bard whispers. You blink twice, your eyes darting this way and that, and realize to your chagrin that she's speaking of you.

"Me?" you mutter. "I—why? There's nothing to sing about."

The bard frowns. "There's always something to sing about. Our own tales are intricate tapestries of the finest silk. We have but to pull a thread."

* * *

Turn to the ordinary.

I never grow tired of hearing the story of the Baptism of Jesus. It's an important tale in my own spiritual growth. My spiritual director long ago pointed to this scene as foundational to the inner life. In typical Ignatian fashion, I was told to place myself in the story, take on the mantle of one of the characters, and feel and taste and see and hear everything that occurred.

What happens at the Baptism of the Lord? Jesus is thrust under the cold waters of the Jordan River. He is making it a point to publicly embrace ritual in all its tactile glory. Being baptized means quite literally being pressed into the stuff of the earth. But then something strange happens. When Jesus emerges from the depths, he hears a voice coming down from heaven. The voice is speaking to him: "You are my beloved Son; with you I am well pleased."[30]

This is the part of the story I was supposed to really put myself into. What would it mean for God to say those words *to me*? Do I feel them to be true? Do I recognize that I am in fact the beloved of God?

Do *you*?

It's so easy to throw up our hands and say, "Sure, God likes me well enough. But I've done some stuff and not done some other stuff and, well, *beloved* is a strong word and . . ." We struggle to realize that ours is a God of pure delight, who simply wants to rejoice in our very being, to sing our song and dance with us. God desires to behold us who are God's very own beloved ones.

But we often throw up a barrier made of false humility, an unhealthy sense of self, an unease with vulnerability, and we keep God's delight at bay. It's overwhelming. A God who delights doesn't need us to constantly second-guess ourselves, to beat ourselves up, to wallow in shame. A God who delights simply *delights*.

We are the ones who think we have done nothing worthy of a song.

The great Canadian Jesuit John English encourages us to pray with what he calls our graced history. He writes, "A series of events becomes graced history when it is approached and understood in terms of God's constant loving presence with each individual and the whole human race."[31] In short, our entire life is our graced history; all we have to do is reflect upon it in the company of our God who delights in us.

"Ah," you say, "but there are those moments when I really messed up."

So?

God shrugs, smiles, gives you a hug.

"We must view God as approving and affirming when we take a spiritual approach to all the events of our life story," Fr. English writes. "Knowing that God regards us with unconditional love enables us to recall all the events of our lives, whether they are positive or negative. With reflection we recognize the unique way God relates to us."[32]

God isn't saying that we can't or shouldn't make up for our mistakes, or keep getting better in areas where we fall short. Of course God desires our full human flourishing; God continues to call us deeper into Godself! But what Fr. English wants us to remember is that we need not fear looking at our past, at our story. God delights when we do. God affirms the very quest we undertake when we delve into the fullness of our selves.

We can be confident that we journey in the company of a God who delights in us. A God who sings our praises and dances to the tune of our unique legacy. God always has a word of joy to share on our behalf. The question is, Do we take the time to listen? Do we even let God speak?

There is a meditation by Fr. Anthony de Mello that I often use when giving retreats and workshops. It's called "The Advent" and it's an invitation to reflect upon God-at-work in our life stories. The entire meditation is beautiful, but one section in particular always seems to get people. I know that it gets me. Near the end of the meditation, de Mello instructs us to "recall the song the angels sang when Christ was born." The radios in our minds instinctively tune to the Christmas channel and we hear angels serenading us with words like "hark" and "joy" and "peace."

But then de Mello turns the tables: "Have I ever heard the song the angels sang when I was born?" he asks. And the answer, from one retreatant to the next, is a resounding stunned and silent *no.* So, I send retreatants off to listen for that song, to see if they can't hear a melody or get down on paper a few grace-filled lyrics.

Because the truth of the matter is this: The angels *did* sing a song for each of us at our birth—a song of joy and wonder and love. Now, we're invited to allow that song to seep into our souls, and then to join in the singing, the dancing, and the delight.

* * *

AND NOW, CROSS THE THRESHOLD THAT LINKS THE ORDINARY TO THE FANTASTICAL.

You're uneasy when the bard begins to sing. You know you've accomplished nothing worthy of a song. You've merely managed to stumble your way from your own front door to someone else's dinner table. Without the kindness of so many strangers, you'd be nowhere—and stuck.

But the bard doesn't give you a chance to say as much. Instead, she begins her song.

"The road lays still and silent
'Til someone steps this way.
Without the fall of heavy feet
The road would soon decay.
So spare a word of kindness
For those who make it past.
But more than kindness, more than praise.
Kinship is what will last.

Doubt not the time you spend here,
Nor who you spend it with.
For many a day gets whittled away
The road is lost to myth."

You lean back in your chair, stunned, humbled, and smiling.

The bard reminds us that our story is a song worth singing and rejoicing in. How often do we listen to it, and what does it sound like when we do?

THE FOURTEENTH CONTEMPLATION

The Winged Terror, or, When Anger Overwhelms

Step into adventure.

There's an odd and sudden wind that causes you to glance upward. You shield your eyes against the setting sun, squinting.

"Is that . . . are those . . . birds?"

Your eyes struggle to make sense of what you're seeing. Silhouettes against the sun, nothing more, but they have the most peculiar shape. Human, yes, but also winged. Their heads—or, where you assume heads to be—are crowned with wriggling curls, dancing this way and that as the creatures soar through the sky.

Soar closer to you, you realize. They're getting bigger, nearly blocking out the sun. And there are three of them, rapidly coming into focus.

The old elf beside you lets out a long sigh. "Not quite birds and not quite women," the elf says, as though apologizing. "You might call them harpies or furies or something else entirely. But what we call them matters less than what they are."

"And what are they?" you ask.

"Angry," the elf says.

The guests are hushed, expectant, attentive. The wind is blowing, still persistent, still cold. You wrap your arms around yourself to try and warm up.

The trio of winged creatures is near now, well within view of everyone. Women, perhaps, but more monster than anything: They have great gray wings sprouting from their backs; their hair appears as angry snakes. Their clothes, nothing more than rags, are torn and dirty. But it's their faces that really draw your attention. Eyes like coal, dark and deep, and their teeth bared, revealing teeth like sharpened crystals. The three visitors are hissing at anyone within earshot.

They alight just beyond where the banquet table ends, causing a stir among the guests, who scramble to put more space between themselves and these winged terrors. But what you notice is that every plant—grass, tree, bush, and flower—within the immediate radius of these unwelcome arrivals has suddenly wilted and turned brown and dusty.

What's more, the food in front of you—what had been a rich chocolate cake topped with three different colors of berries—has turned gray as ash. Pieces splinter off and blow away in the wind.

The old elf, head shaking and brow furrowed, still stands beside you.

"I guess not everyone is welcome here," you whisper.

"Why do you say that?" the elf asks.

"I mean—" You gesture at the winged terrors. "Clearly, they weren't invited. And look what's happened now that they're here. Everyone's trying to escape."

"They're always invited," the elf says. "Always welcome. They're the ones who are unable to take their seats."

TURN TO THE ORDINARY.

Anger is divisive. It throws us off balance. Of course, anger is also quite natural, quite common. We all get frustrated now and again. Simple things like the guy who cut you off on the highway, the customer service rep who was nothing short of incompetent, and the invited guest who was late again can sour our mood and throw off our day. But anger isn't always a bad thing. We talk, too, of righteous anger in response to injustice. Such anger propels us to act for the greater good, to right perceived wrongs.

And yet, I can't help but think that anger needs to be taken seriously and undergo further examination. The great Jesuit priest and founder of Homeboy Industries in Los Angeles, Greg Boyle, offers a countercultural take on anger in his book *Cherished Belonging: The Healing Power of Love in Divided Times.*[33] Because we are all irrevocably and unshakably good, he insists that anger is something to be skeptical of.

"Sometimes we lionize our anger as holy, akin to that righteous rage in which the prophets engaged," Fr. Boyle writes. "Not so fast. The problem with our anger is that, by definition, it makes everything about ME. It can't be. Plus, our anger (again, by definition) has to have a target, a THEM. There is no way around it." He goes on to say, "Precisely because it separates, we know God doesn't share in our fury. Fury sets up tribes and draws lines. God never sees things this way."[34]

Fr. Boyle says that this doesn't mean there isn't good and holy work to do as we upset the status quo both in our communities and in our own lives, "not just to point things out, but to point the way."[35] But how we engage this anger, what we let it *do* to us, is something to be mindful of.

We might think of Jesus in the temple, seemingly angry that money changers have set up camp in this holy space and are making a profit from God's people. "[Jesus] began to drive out those selling and buying there," we read in Mark's Gospel. "He overturned the tables of the money changers and the seats of those who were selling doves." But Jesus isn't consumed by his anger; he doesn't let it dictate his actions or set up an us/them dichotomy. In Scripture, we see that he immediately begins to teach after cleansing the space: "He taught them saying, 'Is it not written: "My house shall be called a house of prayer for all peoples"?'"[36] Jesus not only resists the impulse to rage against those who disagree with him; he also points to the all-inclusive nature of God's love—a love that *includes* the very people he just scolded.

Too often, our anger gets the best of us. We allow it to take over our bodies, govern our decisions, harm our relationships. The Vietnamese Buddhist monk Thich Nhat Hanh says, "When anger manifests in us, we must recognize and accept that anger is there and needs to be tended to."[37] Tending to our anger means reflecting on its source and how it's affecting our judgment and behavior. We cannot pretend anger is not there, nor can we chase it away permanently.

Nhat Hanh writes, "When we embrace anger and take good care of our anger, we obtain relief. We can look deeply into it and gain many insights." One of those insights is a better awareness of how our anger manifests within relationships and community. We are not the only ones who suffer as a result. He continues, "Someone who suffers a lot always makes the people around him or her suffer. He does not know how to manage his suffering, how to embrace and transform it."[38]

Jesus shows us what it means to allow our anger *to point the way.* But when we settle for anger that *points and shames*, we find ourselves paralyzed. When we suffer in this way, when we allow the seed of anger to flourish at the expense of the seeds of peace and love and compassion also buried in the soil of our lives, we inevitably cut ourselves off from those around us. We divide ourselves, whether we mean to or not. We let anger overwhelm and overtake us and we lose sight of the good thing we may hope to attain.

The first step is to forgive ourselves so as to then turn and forgive others. We look to heal and make whole rather than allow anger to fester into unbridled rage.

AND NOW, CROSS THE THRESHOLD THAT LINKS THE ORDINARY TO THE FANTASTICAL.

The winged creatures hiss a while longer as the cold air blows. Clouds block the sun. Then, as suddenly as they appeared, the creatures take flight and are gone, leaving behind an aura of discomfort and a table full of rotten ash.

"You would have let them stay?" you ask incredulously.

"All are welcome," the old elf says once more. "But those sad creatures refuse to believe it. They'd rather mock us from a distance than sit among us. It's only to their great loss. They've become consumed by their rage, unable to even imagine sitting at our table." Another shake of the head and a sigh. "And look what they've left us."

The elf gestures to the banquet table, emptied and desolate. You shiver in spite of yourself and frown. And as the sun disappears, darkness sets in.

Winged terrors swoop down unexpectedly
into our lives, evoking rage and fury
and destruction.
But if we dare to welcome these unwelcome
parts of ourselves and others, to enfold them
in a loving embrace, might we disarm them?

THE FIFTEENTH CONTEMPLATION

The Shadow, or, That Which Covers Us in Darkness

STEP INTO ADVENTURE.

The darkness is all encompassing. What light there had been—what joy and happinesses and delight—seems a distant memory. The gloom rolls through the valley and across the fields like a storm descending from an angry god. It touches everything and contaminates what it touches. It confuses everything and everyone. The shadow has crept into your soul, clogging your body with doubt, paralyzing your limbs with fear. Questions you thought had been answered resurface once more. Why did you decide to embark on this path? You aren't prepared for this. You aren't the right one. You should turn back immediately!

That banquet, those songs—it was all a lie. You look to the foliage all around you and see nothing but dusty gray ash. You stand alone against the encroaching darkness. The whole world is dissolving around you, and you're next.

Your eyes go wide as the long claw of the shadow's hand reaches for you, envelops you, drags you down to nothing and nowhere.

Turn to the ordinary.

We all know what it is to be in a state of desolation. We feel listless, worn down, hopeless. We feel as though God is very distant; perhaps we even question whether God has ever been near at all. Our energy sags along with our spirit, and those things that once delighted us suddenly taste sour in our mouth. We find ourselves paralyzed by fear and doubt, unable to see clearly the road ahead of us and overly preoccupied with the many possible missteps we may have taken in the immediate past or present moment.

Desolation does not necessarily signify something bad. After all, sometimes we need to shake up our own status quo if we are to reach the next level. That means we can't stay in desolation. We need to break through and get back on the path of our life's journey.

But St. Ignatius of Loyola presents us with something of a paradox. He says not to make any major decisions when we are in a state of desolation. The road is clouded; we see nothing but shadow. It is much more difficult to discern what we should do next when we stand surrounded by fog. But since we want and need to break through a state of desolation as quickly as possible, we're tempted to make a rash decision. We take that job because it's there and it's easy. We abandon a relationship because it's grown stale and we desire something fresh. We quit working on a passion project because we feel depleted, and who cares about it anyway?

You get the idea: There are many ways by which we can careen off the path in an unhelpful way while in a state of desolation. The false spirit wishes nothing more than to distract and disorient us in such a moment. But if we need to move quickly to get through desolation *and* we need to avoid making any sudden changes in our lives, then don't we find ourselves at a standstill? Aren't we stuck?

No. The key is to keep moving forward, one steady step at a time. We don't make big changes, but we do take small, consistent steps. We continue to weigh the signs of the times, to look for God's still, quiet voice in the patterns of our lives, even if God feels distant. We engage in the rituals of our days: We pray, we exercise, we spend time with loved ones, we read books and watch movies. We continue living, even if it's hard. Even if all of life's light feels consumed by shadow. Why? Because though God may *feel* distant, God is never any further away than the breath sustaining our bodies. We trust in God's constant, loving presence and delight. And we continue moving along the path God has called us to travel, even if it is temporarily cloaked in darkness.

God is ever faithful. The last right decision you made is still the right decision. Trust in yourself. Trust that God continues to animate your very being. And press on.

The shadow will give way to light.

* * *

AND NOW, CROSS THE THRESHOLD THAT LINKS THE ORDINARY TO THE FANTASTICAL.

"It takes only the smallest of light," a voice whispers in your ear. The spirit guide.

You realize then that your hands are clasping the magic stones; they glow dimly. But they're comfortable in your hands and warm. You take some solace in their familiar shape, smooth and firm. You begin to breathe again.

"Hold fast," the voice whispers again. "Nothing has changed. You are still the same person the bard brought to song, the same person who pressed through the forest. Hold fast and look to the light."

The light, you realize, burns within you.

Shadow inevitably reaches for us throughout our lives.
How can our steadfast routine continue to spark light in us?

THE SIXTEENTH CONTEMPLATION

The Sword, or, That Which Cuts Both Ways

STEP INTO ADVENTURE.

They've invited you down into a dark cellar. It's cold, and the air hangs heavy. Every footfall echoes; every breath is a windstorm. And you've still not reached your destination. But you dare not ask how much further—the moment is too sacred, too poignant.

You're in the center of a procession of seven. There are three elves in front of you and three behind. Their robes flow around their feet as they walk. Their gazes are set on the blazing candles in their hands. You wish you were holding a candle, if only for the small bit of warmth the flame would give. Instead, you clutch your staff with one hand. You find comfort in holding the magic stones—talismans against you know not what—in the other.

"One final gift," the old elf had said to you. But then, with a half-hearted smile, the elf added, "The wizard wants you to have it." You could almost hear the words that were left unspoken: "Just in case." But what it is and why it's needed remains a mystery.

Down, down, down into the depths of the world you go, one unsteady step at a time. You feel the shadow still reaching for you; you can sense it at the edge of your visual field. But it feels good to be moving. It feels good to have direction.

The elves begin to chant. At first, it's a hum, but then it blossoms into words you cannot decipher. Their pace slows. You have no choice but to adjust your own pace.

The procession spills out into a small cavern. Light emanates from the walls and ceiling, evidently a peculiar property of the yellowish moss that covers the stone. The elves fan out, taking up positions around the room. It's only then you notice in the center—

"Truth," the old elf intones, nodding to the sword encased in glass and displayed on a stone altar. "She requires a deft hand. But even—and necessarily—so, she draws as much blood from her master as from any would-be foe."

"Is that the sword's name?" you ask. "Truth?"

The elf only smiles. "The blade is merely a manifestation." Then, silence.

Turn to the ordinary.

When I was in third grade, my grandmother bought me a copy of *The Sword of Shannara*, written by the eminent fantasy author Terry Brooks. It's a classic high fantasy text, a story that derives much of its magic from *The Lord of the Rings.* I loved it. The story holds a premiere place in my own literary history. It was formative, one of the first fantasy novels I read on my own. It felt bigger, too, more grown-up. I proceeded to inhale all of Brooks' *Shannara* books.

I remember talking with a classmate who was also up to her eyes in *The Sword of Shannara*. She loved it, found it enchanting.

"How about the sword?" she said. "Can you believe its power?"

I shrugged. The ending felt anticlimactic to me. "The sword tells the truth," I said, shrugging. "Yeah—it was okay." My friend was aghast.

I remember back then and for many years after thinking that that was the lamest power a weapon could possibly have. The legendary sword of the Elven King Jerle Shannara had the power to expose anyone who touches it to the truth of their lives, the truth about themselves. The Warlock Lord, the villain of the story, had built his entire life's legacy on lies. As soon as the blade touched him, revealing his mortality, revealing that there was in fact nothing to him, nothing for him to cling to that wasn't a falsehood, he was destroyed.

Okay, cool, I'd thought. *But also, couldn't the final confrontation have had more . . . action?*

But way back then, what did I know about truth? How was I to appreciate the profundity of such a weapon? I've long since lost my copy of *The Sword of Shannara*, but the sword itself hangs ever in my mind. I wonder now whether I could withstand its power. What truth would it reveal about me? What gaps in my thinking, what oversights, what sins of omission, what biases and private prejudices? I'm not sure I could handle knowing these things. Not all at once, at least. Such sudden, sweeping knowledge might destroy me.

Just like the Warlock Lord, I've built up an image of myself. I hope it's built on truth, but I am aware that I fall victim to my own delusions, my own ego. The spiritual life, I think, is an invitation to come closer to the truth, to better understand our true selves, the person God knows we are, knows we may yet become. But it also demands that we confront difficult truths about ourselves, that we dismantle the false self and look clearly at who we actually are, what we've actually done, and what we might actually be able to do as we press onward.

Truth is a powerful weapon. But it cuts both ways. It reveals our deepest selves, and that can hurt.

When standing before Pontius Pilate, Jesus says, "For this I was born, and for this I came into the world, to testify to the truth. Everyone who belongs to the truth listens to my voice."

Pilate responds, "What is truth?"[39]

Maybe it's too hard for a man like Pilate. He's built too much of himself on sand, and the truth of who he is will crumble under the weight of itself. I wonder if this is why Jesus invites us to listen to his voice, to belong to him. It sounds like an invitation—an invitation to a journey. We go slowly, steadily. We cannot handle it all at once. Jesus knows this. That's why he is the way and the truth and the life. It's an unfolding invitation. We set out along *the way* to better understand *our own truth* and thus live *the fullest life*. Even though it's not easy and it's not quick and the sharp edge of truth stings, still, we keep going.

AND NOW, CROSS THE THRESHOLD THAT LINKS THE ORDINARY TO THE FANTASTICAL.

You approach the altar, reach out your hand.

"Carefully, now," the old elf says. "Slowly."

You take the glass case from its altar. You place it on the floor at your feet. And then you place your hand on the blade's hilt. It's cool to the touch. You expect something to happen—some blast of air or trumpet's call—but nothing does.

You heft the blade, feel its weight. One of the elves approaches with a scabbard; you sheath the sword and attach it to your hip.

"Nothing happened," you say, turning to the elves gathered. "But thank you all the same. I will protect it."

"Nothing happened, you say?" the old elf whispers. "Think back."

And you do. And you realize that all of your memories feel different, look different. You see new things, new people, new places, and you see them with more clarity than before. You feel new things, too. Your body feels full—too full. You begin to second-guess, think back, reassemble the pieces.

And then you crumble to the ground. It's all too much.

The sword cuts both ways.
Are we able to look plainly at the wounds it exposes in ourselves?

THE SEVENTEENTH CONTEMPLATION

The Vision, or, When the Spiritual and Temporal Meet

STEP INTO ADVENTURE.

Nothing looks right. But everything feels familiar.

You stand in a large field surrounded by people you know. There's a comfort in their presence. Yet, when you look directly into their faces, everything seems off. Their eyes are too big and their mouths too small. They wear funny hats and odd clothing. And everyone is dancing. They leap into the air, twirling and singing, spinning about in a circle.

Where are you? What is this, some sort of ritual? Or, perhaps, a trick? You try to remember back to where you last were, when you last felt the ground firmly beneath your feet, but you can't quite place it and—

And that's when you realize you're floating. Just a few meters above the tilled farmland, but still. Definitely floating.

Your friends and family are dancing nearer now. You realize they are floating, too. And smiling. But their faces are blurred, fuzzy. Nothing is clear.

You realize you feel fuzzy, too. Your head, at least. It's spinning. These people parading around you, they must want something. Need something. They're trying to tell you something, invite you somewhere, entice you to go deeper.

You remember a darkness and you remember a descent and you remember that there is a power in your pocket. This is a memory—you believe it to be, at least—but it feels disconnected. You reach into your pocket, try to discover what power lies therein. But a bird erupts instead, taking to the sky with a powerful flapping of its wings. The wings are blue, you see, and with every tiny movement they emanate a gold glimmery substance, a trail of magic and wonder.

That came from you? You realize then that the people around you have stopped dancing. They are standing still and they are staring. In unison, they point to the bird as it soars above your head and then they point to you.

And you stand—or, float—there, clueless, wondering where you are and what is happening, unsure if any of this is real, but quite sure that it matters.

Turn to the ordinary.

Icons are weird. I say that with deep affection.

One of the priests at my childhood parish gave a different religious icon as a Christmas gift every year. My mom, by virtue of her role as the parish office manager, received each of these annual gifts. They hang in a room in our house. Though my family has no great devotion to icons, they remain there all the same. As a child, I would look at them and wonder. Some seemed like otherworldly profiles. Others depicted scenes I recognized from Scripture, though often in an exaggerated way. One such scene—Abraham unknowingly entertaining angels—felt fantastical in the lopsided scale of its looming, dour figures. All the same, that image and the corresponding biblical verses dug their way into my religious imagination. As a young person, I didn't know quite what to make of these depictions, but I did know that they were important. Significant. Prayerful.

Over time, I grew to love these images, not from any particular sort of piety, or sudden burst of insight, or in-depth academic study. It was more their familiarity. And that scene with the mysterious angelic visitors now hangs in my kitchen as a reminder to practice hospitality.

It wasn't until I interviewed Chris Pramuk, author, professor, and Regis University Chair of Ignatian Thought and Imagination, that I really began to embrace the strangeness of icons. I asked Chris about a particular passage in his book *All My Eyes See: The Artistic Vocation of Fr. William Hart McNichols* because in his younger years, Chris also found icons hard to pray with.

Pramuk's passage that held me in its grip read,

> The faces gazing back at me from their gold-leafed surfaces seemed to me strange and exotic, somewhat rigid, not quite people; to my eyes they were otherworldly, not "realistic," seeming to come, as it were, from the other side. Later I would understand that this visual dissonance is precisely the point, that by their very nature icons attempt to do what is logically impossible: to unite at once the unportrayability and portrayability of God, whose presence is both hidden and manifest in the world.[40]

I had spent years trying to be all delicate and pious, pretending I "got" the spiritual depths of these icons. But Chris said the quiet part out loud! These things are weird, but intentionally so. They're *meant* to be unsettling. They're *meant* to awaken us to the disorienting, unfathomable strangeness of God and God's way. Icons can act as gateways to the supernatural, passages through which we touch the spiritual realm that exists just beyond our fingertips.

Icons *are* fantastical. However, because they are fantastical renderings of stories we know and count as familiar, icons feel like dreams.

Dreams and visions are not in short supply when we look at Scripture. Joseph's dream helps save his family and all of Egypt. The Book of Revelation reads like some twisted, drug-induced hallucination. Saints and mystics throughout time and across all spiritual traditions encounter the Divine through dreams and visions. And so do we.

I'm struck by this line from St. Paul's first letter to the Corinthians: "At present we see indistinctly, as in a mirror, but then face to face. At present I know partially; then I shall know fully, as I am fully known."[41] Paul is reminding us that knowledge and prophesy are known partially, but in the fullness of God's time, when the perfect arrives, we will see all things clearly. Or, we can't know the fullness of the future; all we can do is screw up our face as we try to decipher the signs and patterns at hand. What's important here, Paul emphasizes, is our resolute commitment to love. He says, "So faith, hope, love remain, these three; but the greatest of these is love."[42] That's how he ends the chapter, reminding us that regardless of how clearly we do or do not see, love remains our aim.

What if we looked at our incomplete dreams and our foggy visions, at these images that both confuse and delight, as God's reminder that the work of love is so much greater than we can fully understand? What if we kept in our mind that any invitation into the unknown, into the fantastical, is first and foremost an invitation to love in new and unimaginable ways?

The faces are indistinct, perhaps, because we're called to love whomever we encounter, the familiar and the stranger alike. Love is the guiding light that ultimately disperses that fog and reveals God's glory.

***

AND NOW, CROSS THE THRESHOLD THAT LINKS THE ORDINARY TO THE FANTASTICAL.

And then, as though from within your very self, a warm light begins to glow. The bird vanishes on the horizon, but its gleaming trail continues to illuminate the amber field. All those people gathered around you continue to point to you.

Or . . . are they pointing to something within you?

Either way, any discomfort has dissipated, all uncertainty has fallen away. And then the faces begin to take on a new clarity, but just as soon as you look into the eyes of those around you, the warmth overwhelms you and—

The vision is gone. But the shimmering feeling, the warmth, somehow remains.

Embracing the strangeness of a vision can help us assume a disposition that embraces a God beyond our wildest imagining.
Are we able to dwell in the realm of such strange and wondrous power?

THE EIGHTEENTH CONTEMPLATION

The Words of Power, or, Why Bother with a Blessing

STEP INTO ADVENTURE.

The humming again, low and insistent. You can feel it in your body. Your skin vibrates to its pitch; your teeth seem to tingle. The sensation has you under its spell, a grip you cannot shake. It's pulling you out of . . . out of . . .

Words are crystalizing, clarifying, concretizing.

"You who have been pulled beyond, look back to where you began. You who have been cast aside, stand back where you belong. You who have been left in doubt, shed the skin of lies."

The words are pungent and thick, like an ointment. They sink deep into your muscles.

"You who have been made to wander, stop and take your rest. You who have been lost in fog, feel the clean wind disperse the mist."

Your limbs, your head, your feet feel heavy. But then you realize that it's only because you had been floating before; you've returned to the flesh and bone and blood that make you you.

"You who have been bound by sleep, awaken." Your eyes flutter open, and you remember.

Turn to the ordinary.

The retreat master at the monastery I was visiting was an old monk named Damian. Every day he met the retreatants in the common room to offer a few words of reflection that were intended to be raw material for our daily prayer. His voice, quiet and confident, was the only voice we heard during our silent retreat.

On the very first day, almost as an afterthought before sending us on our way, he offered to give our small group a blessing. To be honest, I can't remember the exact words, but this was the essence of what he said: "Always take a blessing when it's offered. Always. It's good energy. It's good for you. It's simply one person reminding you that God is here and God's Spirit goes with you. That God loves you. Always allow another person to bless you with God's Spirit."

I remember he made it quite clear that the religious background we associated with didn't matter to him. For Fr. Damian, it was all about accepting a blessing, accepting God's Spirit, allowing one person to transmit to another something of the sacred. It was a simple, powerful opportunity to remind ourselves that the veil between the secular and the sacred is thin, and it can be pierced with but a few words.

I think of Fr. Damian whenever I receive a blessing. His understanding of this simple, holy act felt so accessible, approachable, down-to-earth. And yet, what he was insisting upon was that what we were doing was otherworldly. We were transmitting and receiving the Spirit; we were allowing our bodies to be vessels through which words conveyed supernatural meaning, which is to say meaning that could reshape our reality. And why? So that we could remind one another that God was really here, that God's Spirit was really with us, that God's own self journeyed with each of us, God's own beloved.

Is that hard to hear? Is it hard to receive a blessing—or even just a kind word, or an affirmation of work done well or a skill well used—because we shrink at the sound of someone reminding us of our own belovedness, our own worth and wonder?

I know how often I bow my head and raise my hand in disagreement as I dismiss words of affirmation. Do we do the same thing to God's own Spirit, the Spirit of Life that desires to dwell and delight in us? Do we deflect the graces that God desires to shower upon us? I think of the words of seventh-century hermit and saint Isaac the Syrian. "Let your mouth constantly speak words of blessing; then the scorn of another will never hurt you," he says. Why? Because when our disposition is one of blessing, negativity and judgment more readily roll off of us. We look first for the good so as to celebrate it instead of seeking out the shortcomings in another for the sole purpose of judgment and one-upmanship. When we sink into the waters of disdain, we become trapped in a vicious cycle. Isaac the Syrian continues, "Disdain gives birth to disdain, blessing to blessing."[43] Let us be founts of blessing, not drains of despair.

Monsignor Philip Ricci, the pastor at my childhood parish, often bestowed upon our congregation the Aaronic Blessing. So significant is this blessing to me that we asked that Monsignor Ricci bless my wife and me with the Aaronic Blessing at our wedding. Drawn from the book of Numbers, the Lord tells Moses how to instruct Aaron and his sons in blessing the Israelites:

May the Lord bless you. May the Lord keep you.
May he show his face to you and have mercy.
The Lord bless you; the Lord keep you.
May he turn to you his countenance and give you peace.
The Lord bless you.

This blessing expresses a great desire that God turn God's own face to gaze upon us, and in that gazing, bring us peace. As we bless one another and recognize that we are all made in the image and likeness of God, let us pray that our gazes transmit peace. Might that be our blessing? We give and receive the peace of God, peace that reconciles us to the world but also reconciles us to ourselves, to past moments that may be hard to swallow but that make us who we are all the same.

God looks upon us in all we have been, all we are, all we are yet to be, and delights. This is the wondrous truth that a blessing transmits.

Who *wouldn't* want one?

AND NOW, CROSS THE THRESHOLD THAT LINKS THE ORDINARY TO THE FANTASTICAL.

"Welcome back," the old elf says. "You were gone for some time."

"I was . . ." You pause. "I was remembering. I think."

"And it is good to do so. But sometimes we get stuck in the past. Sometimes we need to be returned to our present."

"Whatever you did, whatever you said, it brought me back."

The old elf nods. "Because, ultimately, it is here when you belong."

You raise an eyebrow. The peculiar word choice was not lost on you. "Where?" you suggest.

"Where is what happens next," the old elf says with a smile. Another elf steps forward, helps you up. A third hands you your staff. You check to be sure the sword is secure at your hip and pat your pocket to confirm that the stones are there.

"This is where we part ways," the elf says. "Your path lies deeper still." The elf gestures down a cavernous tunnel you could've sworn wasn't there a moment earlier. The elf takes you by the shoulders, looks you straight in the eye. "Go in peace," the elf says.

You can feel the weight of those words, the truth therein. They give you strength.

The words of power remind us who we are,
whose we are, and set us on our way.
What blessing still rings in our ears?

THE NINETEENTH CONTEMPLATION

The Minotaur, or, The Maze That Traps Us

STEP INTO ADVENTURE.

You realize that you're running. Your boots slam against the hardened ground. You're not sure when your steady walk accelerated into a brisk stroll into a light jog into this current mad dash. All you know is that your breath comes in shallow, rapid bursts. Your staff keeps bumping into the narrowing cavern walls. The lichen that's lit so much of your path grows more sparsely here. The shadow is quite literally lengthening all around you.

You pause for just a moment. Maybe it's all in your head. Maybe the noise that caused you to increase your pace was really nothing. Maybe you're letting your imagination get the better of you. After all, why would you be sent into a cavernous maze that was already home to a—

Your rumination is interrupted by noises. You can no longer pretend you don't hear the steady clamor of hooves. You can no longer dismiss the angry, haggard breathing. You can no longer ignore what sounds like a battle-ax bashing into the rocky walls as its bearer barrels toward you.

That's it, you think. I have to make a stand. I have to face whatever this is. You draw your sword, taking momentary solace in the ringing sound it makes when freed from its sheath. But whatever comfort you found dissipates when you see the saber shaking in the dim light. Shaking in your poorly trained hands.

That's when the minotaur appears.

"Game over," it snarls. "You've been caught."

The monster had been running at a terrifying pace, but even more frightening is its sudden, skidding halt. Its hooves dig into the ground; its bullish horns rake against one side of the tunnel. With its muscular arms it buries its battle-ax deep into the ground, scattering broken stone and debris that fly up at your face. Then it grins—an unnatural and unnerving expression for a half-bull, half-human creature.

The minotaur stands to its full height and hefts the axe on its shoulder. Its eyes are red; its upper body all twisted animal muscle and fur. Its head looks like a demon bull; its body like the discarded remains of a once-mighty knight. And the hooves: they step left and right, back and forth, constantly moving, never not in motion.

The monster is ugly, unnatural, twisted, and sick. You take a tentative step back, lean heavily on your staff, and do your best to brandish your blade. You blink once. Twice. As though the beast will vanish if you just give it time.

"Now I bury you in the darkness," the creature laughs. "Rip up your body, leave your entrails on these cavern walls." Gurgling laughter. "My axe and your neck."

TURN TO THE ORDINARY.

The minotaur is a monster sentenced to live out its days trapped in a labyrinth from which it cannot escape. Why was it given this particular punishment? As the offspring of lust and trickery and unnatural desire, the minotaur is an abomination and must be punished accordingly. Or so say the myths.

The minotaur is a sick and twisted thing that preys on human flesh. One is left to wonder, though: Does it look upon its victims with envy? Does it wish for the purity of the human form, as it sees it? Does it see reflected in its victim's eyes its own beastly self? Because the minotaur represents something important. In this monster, we're tempted to see that which we fear we might become if we let our truest selves rage unchecked. We are, after all, only animals. We are all half beast. Within each of us is a monster.

Whenever we encounter creatures such as this, we should pause and look inward. Is there some perverse hatred of the human form—*our* human form—that gives rise to these imaginings? What is the disdain for our *creatureliness* that dubs such beings "monsters?" We dislike being associated with animals, particularly as we see these so-called animal instincts within ourselves.

And yet, we eat and drink and make love and run and jump and sweat, not because we are weak but because we are human. We are part of the world, part of creation. There's no need to see these parts of ourselves as less than. This isn't a *monster* living within us; it's simply a part of us, and it might be there to remind us that we all are in need of love. Rather than shame it and hide it away, could we let the beast free and allow it to take its place in creation?

We can never be reminded too many times that God became human, and that the Incarnation—the literal *embodiment* of God—is foundational to our faith. Jesus was seen "coming in human likeness; and found human in appearance."[44] This is meant to serve as validation that the fullness of our humanity is sacred because it's the very nature into which God chose to enter. The Incarnation is instrumental to our salvation; through it, we are reassured that our body and soul have value in God's eyes.

Jesus spit in the mud and Jesus touched wounded flesh. Jesus walked for miles and rested when necessary. Jesus embraced his friends and wept for those who were lost. God, through Jesus, was fully embodied, and we are made in the image and likeness of this same God who calls all created things *good*.

And yet, how often do I look in the mirror and scowl at my gut and graying hair? How often do I castigate myself for getting winded while I am running? How often do I wring my hands over one-too-many cookies? How often do you?

Is this the minotaur living within each of us? Is the minotaur that bit of flab, that bulging gut, that unsightly mole or receding hairline, or is it our obsession over these imperfections? Do we dub these things ugly and inadequate so that we can make them into figurative monsters to be slain? Is this the lesson of the minotaur? Because if it is, we really do spend a lifetime wandering the minotaur's labyrinth in search of perfection we'll never achieve. Our bodies will never be perfect because perfection will always be one push-up away. It's a goal we can never reach. What we can do, though, is follow after our God. We can be someone who is grateful to have a body that can breathe the fresh air and taste the salt of the ocean and feel the strain of tired muscles. Rather than punish this body, we should delight in it and use it to get up and go about the work of redemption. God became human not to call us ugly but to behold us and cherish us as beloved.

And now, cross the threshold that links the ordinary to the fantastical.

You continue to hold your blade in front of you even though all the while you're stumbling backwards. The minotaur is licking its lips, tightening its grasp on the wicked handle of its axe. The cavern feels smaller, as though it's beginning to squeeze the very life out of you.

You adjust your hold on your sword, and suddenly a wave of insight washes over you. Your eyes go wide. The sword's hidden power seeps into your mind and then emanates from every pour in your body.

You can tell the minotaur sees it, too. The beast stops its forward press, though its restless hooves continue stomping the stone and dirt.

You tilt your head to one side, squinting as you look at the minotaur anew. There's still fear and worry and anger boiling in your gut, but a new emotion rises: curiosity. Words bubble to your lips. "The labyrinth," you say. "It's unending, and yet you still feel trapped."

"Silence," the minotaur growls. "I'll rip your tongue—"

"For all the space you have here, it's not yours. Not really. It's a trap—a prison. You just want to feel . . ."

The minotaur bares its teeth, makes as though to lunge.

"Belonging. You want to feel as though you've been invited in, not captured."

At those words, the minotaur lets out a mighty bellow, a sound at the intersection of a roar and a scream. Then it turns and runs away, vanishing back into the shadows from which it appeared.

You nod. "Well, then," you say, and exhale. You sheath your sword, steady your staff, and continue walking. "Let's see what else is in here."

**The minotaur lives in each of us.
What do we need to do to free it
from its labyrinthine prison?**

THE TWENTIETH CONTEMPLATION

The Cave, or, Facing Our Shadow Selves

STEP INTO ADVENTURE.

Down, down, down you go. The tunnels seem to have no end. The cave is bigger than you dared imagine, each tunnel spilling into a new cavernous chamber. You have no idea how far you need to travel; you can barely remember how long you've been walking. But you continue all the same, one foot in front of the other, trusting that you're headed somewhere and that the slight wind at your back and the glowing lichen growing along the path will lead you to wherever that somewhere might be.

You do not travel alone, though.

"Why didn't they tell me where to go?" your doubt worries aloud. "What if this is a dead end and we have to circle back? What if we get trapped—or worse?" You look at your doubt and scowl.

"How dare they trap me here with that monster," your anger fumes. "A minotaur of all things! Those fool elves sent me here to die." Steam emanates from your anger; you can see it streaming upward in the shadows.

"I bet the others the wizard selected had an easier time," your envy opines. "I bet they didn't have to go through this dreadful cave. I bet they had magic or an army or, or, or—something better."

"I bet they had better food," your hunger whines, having all but forgotten the glorious feast.

"I bet they had a place to rest," your weariness yawns.

"I just can't imagine we're ever going to get anywhere," your anxiety stammers. "This staff is all but useless, these stones in our pocket are basically just paperweights and no one taught us how to wield a sword! We're never going to get out of this alive. Oh—why did we agree?"

"None of it matters because we're not worthy of reaching the end anyway," your shame whispers. "After all the failures we've had? No. Not worthy at all. We're better off staying in these shadows and never leaving."

When you burst from one tunnel into the next cavern, you realize how crowded the place suddenly feels. You glance around and see all sorts of images of yourself: some bold and brave, others tired and defeated. Some overweight; others malnourished. And more: one scowling, another whimpering, another simply blank-faced and still.

"Quiet, all of you!" you scream. But there's no reaction. The voices only grow in volume. Finally, you brandish the blade, hopeful that the truth will set you free. But as you swing the sword at one image after another, all they do is turn to you and laugh.

"This is your truth," one says. "We are who you are."

✷✷✷

Turn to the ordinary.

I met a friend for coffee one afternoon at a café near my home. Lattes in hand, we retreated to a pair of chairs at the rear of the restaurant, hoping to find some privacy to talk.

"I'm feeling angry all the time," I confessed.

"There's a Buddhist parable on anger," my friend said. "Have you heard it?"

I said I had not, and so he shared. The story goes something like this:

A monk boards a boat to meditate in private in the middle of the lake. While he is sitting on the boat, enjoying a time of silence and reflection, another boat bumps into his. The monk opens his eyes, turning in anger to scold the foolish captain of this wayward vessel, saying, "Can't you see I'm meditating? You have the whole lake on which to sail! Give me my space!" But as he turns toward the offending ship to address its incompetent captain face-to-face, he sees that the boat is empty. It had detached itself from the dock and now was floating aimlessly, without a crew. There was no one on it. So, no one had bumped into the monk. There was no one to be angry with. How foolish to yell at wind and waves!

The now-enlightened monk realized that his anger did not originate from *beyond* the monk but from *within*. It was and always had been part of him. It was his to own, and his to tend.

The motif of the cave in the spiritual life is both important and helpful. In my mind, caves quickly conjure the scene in *Star Wars: Episode V—The Empire Strikes Back*, when Luke Skywalker enters the dark side cave on the swamp planet Dagobah. He asks his teacher, Yoda, "What's in there?" Yoda replies, "Only what you take with you."

When Luke encounters a vision of Darth Vader in the cave, he strikes down the Dark Lord with his buzzing lightsaber, only to find that beneath Vader's mask is Luke's own face. So, what did Luke bring with him into the cave? He brought his own fears and doubts, his own worries that he would fall to the same evil that had claimed Vader.

The cave shows up in the story of St. Ignatius of Loyola, too. In a cave near Manresa, Spain, Ignatius spends eleven months in prayer. There, he documents the movements of the Spirit in his prayer life—what ultimately becomes his *Spiritual Exercises*, a great wisdom text that has changed the lives of people the world over. But it's also in that cave that the false spirit tempts him. The false spirit insists that Ignatius is not enough, that there's no way he can live out the life God has called him to live. We can only imagine that the false spirit puts in Ignatius's mind images of himself failing, falling short, giving up, and going home. Here in this cave, Ignatius suffers such a profound sense of desolation that he considers taking his own life.

The cave motif appears in spiritual traditions the world over. These are pressure cooker moments for the spiritual life. These are the times when we come face-to-face with our own doubts. We see versions of ourselves that make us uncomfortable. We see our own challenges exaggerated to a troubling degree. We feel crestfallen at falling so short of who we think we are, or who we'd like to become. Tempted to fight those other selves, we fail to realize that these are just parts of who we fully are. We don't fight them; we reconcile and make ourselves whole.

In our own cave moments, we come up against our supposed failings, sure. But we're also given the opportunity to recognize that we are more than just our individual parts. Our parts are important because each part serves a purpose. They protect us, guide us, keep us vigilant. But they must be integrated, welcomed. Only in our fullness can we become the person God invites us to be.

Whether we're a monk on a boat or a Jedi in a cave, we must face the storms of emotions bubbling within us. The false spirit would distract us, casting shadows on darkened walls for us to chase. How much easier it is to slay an external villain than to look deep within and make peace with our own wounds, with our own less-than-savory parts! But this is precisely why we enter the cave. We must see all those seemingly disparate parts of ourselves and love them into wholeness. Every part is important.

* * *

AND NOW, CROSS THE THRESHOLD THAT LINKS THE ORDINARY TO THE FANTASTICAL.

You realize you cannot go on like this. There is too much chatter, too much noise, too much confusion. And no one is in charge of any of it.

"Wait," you say suddenly. All of your heads turn to look at you. "I'm in charge of all of it. It's all me. It's all necessarily me."

You sit there on the cavern floor, cross-legged and with your staff on your knees. You hold the magic stones in your hand, breathing deeply, feeling their smooth, firm texture.

"I'm in charge," you breathe in. "It's all me." You exhale. Then: "Thank you," you breathe in. "It's all me." On the exhale, you open an eye. The cavern is empty. And you smile.

They're all still there, within you—you can feel them, sense them, hear them. But it's quieter, more peaceful. You've given them their space. And in time, they give to you their stories, each of these pieces of yourself. You've not silenced or suppressed them; you've embraced them. Each will inevitably have a part to play in your unfolding adventure.

The cave is a pressure cooker of emotions, feelings, desires, and fears.
How can we embrace and integrate these parts of ourselves into wholeness?

THE TWENTY-FIRST CONTEMPLATION

The Undead, or, Our Necessary Reminder

Step into adventure.

The procession began in silence. You would have missed it entirely if not for the tickling chill of an icy breath on your neck. You shivered, swatting at the space between your shoulders, hoping to make contact with a pesky bug. Instead, the cold air took your hand and spun you around, and now you are staring into an underground chamber lit by a yellow glow with no obvious source, though you have little time or lasting interest in seeking out the unseen lamp.

There are too many ghosts.

Every shape, every size, all made of some otherworldly plasma, some greenish, transparent, misty goo. They float along, bouncing on the unseen air, beginning in the shadowy distance on your left and proceeding with haphazard determination into the shadowy distance on your right. They glimmer in and out of this plane, suddenly there and suddenly gone. Some shamble onward with great difficulty dragging a leg or half a tail, though none fully touch the stone and earth of the cavern's floor. Some of the specters have obvious wounds—eyes dangling from sockets, missing arms, heads held tenderly in fingerless hands—while others seem, well, intact.

None make eye contact with you. For that, you are grateful.

That's when you hear the rattling. It sounds like dozens of dried bones put into a tin container and shaken with abandon. And that's not far off from what you're looking at.

There are skeletons now intermingled among the specters. Boney creatures shake and stumble forward. They aren't human—or, they aren't human shaped. Some of the skeletons resemble a human form, but most appear randomly assembled, resembling no living creature you can put a name to. They hover in the air; they drag themselves across the ground; they cling to one another as they make their way in the procession.

The ghosts and specters and skeletal remains hobble in this dark and disturbing parade. You observe it all from a distance, and feel something in your own tired bones cry out, something in your own weary skin tremble.

You wonder whether your eyes have fallen upon the sacred or the profane.

* * *

Turn to the ordinary.

The task at hand was to film a skull. Well, half a skull. The other half was decidedly somewhere else. And when I say "task," I mean I was being paid; like, this was—this *is*—my full-time professional job. I was in New York City at St. Patrick's Cathedral to come up with some sort of video capturing the final stage of the pilgrimage of the skull of the seventeenth-century Jesuit priest, missionary, and martyr St. Jean de Brébeuf.

Well, again, it was just *half* the skull. But they had made a convincing doppelgänger for the other half, so it looked like the real thing. The *whole* thing.

Jean de Brébeuf is one of the eight North American Martyrs, a group of Jesuit missionaries who devoted their lives to working with Indigenous communities of North America. In Brébeuf's case, this work was done in Canada. For his work, and for giving up his life for the sake of the Gospel, Brébeuf was canonized and made a saint. In the Catholic tradition, we look to saints for inspiration in our own spiritual journeys, and we ask saints to pray with us and for us as we muddle our way through life. The custom of venerating their remains began in the earliest days of Christianity. Relics can be pieces of clothing that a saint wore, a piece of fabric or jewelry that touched their skin, some physical object intimately associated with that saint's life or, as in this case, the physical remains of the saint himself.

Brébeuf's skull, displayed in communities across the United States, was drawing a crowd. Folks who came to stand or kneel before the skull and pray walked away with a prayer card that had been touched to Brébeuf's remains. Masses were said, intentions were offered, tears were shed.

There I sat, documenting the whole thing with my camera.

When the video was released, I received criticism from all quarters. There were folks who were upset that the skull had been moved at all: "How can you separate the skull from the rest of the body? Why not let the body rest in peace?"

They had a point.

Others were enraged that I dared film people at prayer: "These people are speaking directly to God by way of this saint's holy remains! How dare you interfere?"

They had a point, too.

Still others curled their lips in distaste and shook their heads in disapproval: "That's so weird. Grotesque, even. You Catholics."

Once more, I had to admit their point was well taken.

But something holy was happening all the same. People gathering to pray, summoned together out of the isolation of their individual lives, their attention drawn not just to the unsettling earthly remains of a long-dead man but simultaneously pointed upward and outward to God's grace and a life that sought the holy in all things and the good in all people. Even from the grisly side of death, God's Holy Spirit was at work. These holy remains dared us to look beyond our present moment and grapple with uncomfortable questions. We were being invited to consider our own mortality and the ultimate meaning of our inevitable death.

In the book of Ezekiel, we experience the prophet's vision of dry bones. He looks out and over a broad valley filled with them! Dry, dusty, and oh-so-dead. "Can these bones come back to life?" God asks. Ezekiel replies, "Lord God, you alone know that."[45] God gives a knowing wink. *Well, then, let's get to prophesizing!*

> Thus says the Lord God to these bones: Listen! I will make breath enter you so you may come to life. I will put sinews on you, make flesh grow over you, cover you with skin, and put breath into you so you may come to life. Then you shall know that I am the Lord. [Ezekiel] prophesized as [he] had been commanded. A sound started up . . . rattling like thunder. The bones came together, bone joining to bone.[46]

This is a startling scene. What began as lifeless dust has suddenly been reborn. A few faith-filled words summoned life from what was incontrovertibly dead. But what strikes me about this scene is that God is not doing a magic trick. God is connecting the past and the present. God is breaking down the thin veil that separates *now* from *eternity.*

The bones *always* pointed beyond what they were. They always pointed toward God, toward what God desired, toward what might yet be. We're temped to cry out, "Our bones are dried up, our hope is lost, and we are cut off!"[47] But God says *no.* God says, *There is more here than meets the eye. The veil is thin between life and death; there is but one great narrative thread, and your story is an essential part.*

Memento mori is Latin for "remember you will die." In his Spiritual Exercises, St. Ignatius of Loyola invites retreatants to do exactly that as they consider decisions to be made. For Ignatius, this death-bed meditation is a way to look with clarity at the options before us. His process for making these decisions is to "consider, as if I were at the point of death, what procedure and norm I will at that time wish I had used in the manner of making the present election. Then, guiding myself by that norm, I should make my decision on the whole matter."[48]

This suggests that Ignatius is inviting us to look at the fullness of our stories as well as at our ultimate destination. We are made for God. We are set here on earth to flourish by giving God glory and serving God's creation. The question then becomes *How*? What "procedures" or "norms" do we know to be important? What values underpin our character? Through what patterns does God most clearly work in our days? In that final moment when we ourselves are about to cross from life to death, how will we feel about the ways in which we acted? Decided? Loved?

We cannot always choose what we do or what happens to us but we can choose how we respond. Do we live well? With hope? With joy? Or with fear, anxiety, and suspicion? These questions beg to be answered because there is much at stake. If we allow fear to lay claim to our lives, how free are we to enter into death?

Yes, those rattling bones of Ezekiel and the half skull of Jean de Brébeuf and any reminder of those who have gone before us are discomforting, and rightly so. We can dismiss these tangible remains as remnants of lives long gone, or we can see them as something more. Something that is speaking to us. The bones invite us to consider what comes next and, essentially, how we choose to live our lives in the meantime.

* * *

AND NOW, CROSS THE THRESHOLD THAT LINKS THE ORDINARY TO THE FANTASTICAL.

"We should move on from this place," the spirit guide whispers in your ear.

"It's like a parade," you say. "I just . . . I can't take my eyes away from it."

"Death is dazzling," is the response. "But worry not, you're in the same parade. You're already marching, though I see still trying to sort out exactly how."

You look around, worried. You try to make eye contact with your familiar, but the creature has not deigned to make itself seen. Instead your eyes fall on darkness.

All the same, you hear a chuckle. "That's why we have parades: to remind ourselves that we're all already in one. And that we march to an inevitable end. But not yet."

Ghosts call out to us from the other side to remind us that life and death are intrinsically connected. How does such a reminder stir us to live more boldly in the present?

THE TWENTY-SECOND CONTEMPLATION

The Djinn, or, Why We Can't Rely Solely on Wishes

Step into adventure.

Along your path lies a grotto, a hidden recess of stone and rock and shadow. You wouldn't have even noticed it had you not paused to wipe the sweat pooling at the back of your neck. You took a deep breath, readjusted your pack, and just so happened to glance to your left.

And there it was: a small cavity punched into the rock wall. You cock your head to the right, wondering. You feel you should keep moving. You need to get out of this cave. The air is lighter here, warmer. The exit is close, and everything about these cavernous tunnels screams at you to get out.

And yet . . .

You take a cautious step toward the stony inlet. Something is calling to you. You've come this far. Why not stop and investigate? You see that there is more to this alcove, that it's worth a brief pause.

Is that an altar set up in the darkness? You step closer, feeling the tightness of the space pressing against you. You lean your staff against the wall outside the small space; you set your sword down behind you. You pull the pouch from your pocket and roll the stones between your fingers, grateful for the lift you get from the mysterious light they provide.

Yes—that is an altar, small but important. It's made of a different kind of stone, something smooth and cream-colored and solid. You place your hand on its surface and are surprised to feel warmth.

And what's this? As you hold your magic stones high, a bluish light leaks through your fingers and you glimpse an amulet cupped in a small marble chalice that is ensconced in the wall above the altar. Your fingers trace text etched into the wall itself.

"To wear this amulet is to bear the One with power to grant life's greatest wish."

You extend your hand toward the amulet, studying its greenish hue, wondering what sort of wishes you might see granted. You glimpse your own reflection there in the amulet, reaching back.

No. Not a reflection.

Something is in the amulet, floating in its emerald mists. Someone. And that someone is reaching toward you.

TURN TO THE ORDINARY.

Disney's 1992 animated movie *Aladdin* was a mainstay of my childhood. I still contend it is one of the best of the Disney animated films. Robin Williams as the Genie? Come on. The greatest!

One of the iconic songs from that movie is "Friend Like Me." You remember it—Aladdin meets the Genie, and the Genie proceeds to lay down the rules of making wishes via a catchy earworm. Genie insists that Aladdin has never had a friend like him, and of course he's right! It's not commonplace to stumble upon a being who can grant (nearly) any wish! It's telling that the song is framed through the lens of friendship. Friendship implies relationship, collaboration, and care for the other person. Both friends in a friendship should desire the full flourishing of the other. As the story progresses, we see Aladdin wrestle with whether to free Genie. Doing so would be an act of true love, one that involves personal sacrifice, especially since to free Genie means to use up a wish.

What about our villain, Jafar? He would make Genie his slave. He doesn't care about Genie; all he cares about is his power. He wants to accrue as many wishes as possible, turning himself into a sorcerer and then an evil genie just to procure might and security. He wants his reign to go on forever. This is a kids movie and the point is obvious. In sacrificing some of his own power, some of his own security, Aladdin frees Genie. In putting someone else first, Aladdin serves a greater good. In contrast, Jafar, who desires only to build up his own power and influence, destroys himself and ends up isolated and empty-handed.

Turns out it's not about the wishes; it's about the relationships.

Dr. Jason T. Eberl, professor and director of the Albert Gnaegi Center for Health Care Ethics at Saint Louis University, was my guest for an episode of "AMDG: A Jesuit Podcast." Jason and I met at a *Star Wars* academic conference at DePaul University; before that meeting, he very kindly wrote an endorsement for my 2024 book, *My Life with the Jedi: The Spirituality of Star Wars*. And well before that, I was reading Jason's philosophical and ethical insights in one of the many pop culture and philosophy volumes he's edited (including *Star Wars and Philosophy*, *Star Trek and Philosophy*, and so on). With this history, I knew he and I were going to get along.

Jason confirmed my hunch when, as preparation for our podcast conversation, he sent me several essays he'd written exploring the ethical implications of *Star Trek* plot points vis-à-vis transhumanism.

Transhumanism as a concept, I soon learned, exists on a wide spectrum. The term encompasses a person taking medication to help focus their mind before a big math test, all the way to someone who has turned themselves into a cyborg (a.k.a. a person who is augmented by robotics). The key element of transhumanism is a desire to use science and technology to improve humanity. *Star Trek*, of course, features actual cyborgs, but more importantly wrestles with the question of what it means to be fully human. For example, can Data, an android, exhibit human qualities? What do we owe The Doctor—an Emergency Medical Hologram—in *Star Trek: Voyager*? The list goes on.

Dr. Eberl suggested two elements that are essential to our humanity: vulnerability and finitude. The latter, of course, means we will one day die; our lives as we experience them here and now will end. (Death, for some transhumanists, is the ultimate boogeyman; these folks are constantly wondering how humanity might evolve past it.) Finitude evokes vulnerability: There are things that can do us harm, that can quite literally end us. These two features seem to go hand in hand.

But vulnerability goes beyond life and death. There are many ways in which we may wish to make ourselves less vulnerable that have nothing to do with dodging the Grim Reaper's scythe. Simply admitting we need help studying for the above-mentioned math test is an act of vulnerability, as is taking the necessary steps to help accomplish that task. Recognizing our own inherent limitations, admitting to our flaws, accepting our wounds—these are all things that make us vulnerable.

I'm not going to litigate the virtues and pitfalls of transhumanism. It's enough to say that I find myself returning to this idea of vulnerability-as-essential to what it means to be human. Here's why: Vulnerability necessitates other people. It thrusts us into the arms of someone else. Into relationship. Vulnerability is a public acknowledgment that I don't have all the answers and I can't do this all on my own. I need someone else. And from out of this recognition, community is born.

Let's tease out the opposite. If we resist vulnerability, if we try to evolve beyond our wounds and weaknesses and necessary limitations, I wonder if we find ourselves increasingly isolated. Do we, perhaps unintentionally, say to others when we avoid sharing our vulnerabilities, "I don't really need or trust or accept you?" Do we close ourselves off, make of ourselves mini gods, dependent on nothing and no one? Do we stop failing and consequently stop growing?

Transhumanism is a spectrum, and there's a lot of good to be found along that spectrum. Using the tools of science, technology, and medicine to help us reach our fullest potential is a great goal. And in fact, the act of recognizing that need, of asking for help and support to reach that full potential is an act of vulnerability. Reaching our potential and cutting ourselves off from our wounds are different things. But both can be goals of a transhumanist perspective. And so we have to ask ourselves: What are we truly after? What do we really want? To discover our deepest selves, or to avoid all possibility of pain?

What was the original sin of Adam and Eve? I'm neither a theologian nor a biblical scholar, but I am struck by the stated desire to "be like gods."[49] To my contemporary ears, that sounds an awful lot like an attempt to short-circuit human vulnerability. How often in our days do we reach for metaphorical apples, hoping they'll keep us from having to look clearly at our own limited selves, our own human frailties, our own wounds? How often do we pretend at being greater than we are so as to avoid the necessity of having to deepen our relationships? Said more plainly, how often do we pretend to be invincible when we should really be asking for help?

God doesn't want to be usurped; God wants to be with us on the journey. We might hear in that catchy *Aladdin* tune God's own self singing to us: *You've never had a friend like me!* Rather than wish our way out of our problems, out of our necessary limitations, why not throw ourselves on our God who desires nothing more than to behold and delight in us?

And now, cross the threshold that links the ordinary to the fantastical.

Your hand reaches for the amulet; the shadow hand reaches back. Your mind races with all the wonderful wishes you might have fulfilled: a quick end to your meandering quest; companionship in place of loneliness; true magic rather than these clumsy stones; a legacy you can be proud of.

But then your hand stops, even as the shadow hand keeps reaching through the amulet. You slowly draw your hand back.

Your mind turns to the countless individuals who have helped you along your way: the elves and the bard, the centaur and the spirit guide; your friends back home and the wizard you pursue even now. An easy out might have made those relationships unnecessary; it might mean you miss the ones yet to come. You don't want that.

"No," you whisper. "I don't need a shortcut. I've come this far."

You turn suddenly, collect your staff and your sword, and march on through the tunnel. You don't look back. Nothing can deter you now. Not even the quiet scream hissing from the emerald amulet.

The djinn's wishes are a shortcut. As we reflect back on our lives, who and what might we have missed if we'd taken such a path?

THE TWENTY-THIRD CONTEMPLATION

The Witches, or, Spiritual Experiences We Don't Understand

Step into adventure.

You emerge from the cavernous maze of winding tunnels into a gray daylight. You shield your eyes all the same; the scene at hand is disconcerting. It becomes obvious that you no longer stand in the elven forest when your boots sink into the muck of a marsh.

The marshland sits nestled in the shade of the mountain. The mountain stands at your back. Crawling in the bog at your feet is a bed of thick, viny grass that reaches out as far as your eyes can see which, due to the rolling mist, is not terribly far. You do note the army of crooked, leafless trees gasping out of the mud, skeletal arms reaching for sunlight as though for the last time.

You listen for birdsong but you hear none. You listen for the scurrying of tiny furry paws but that too is absent. You search the ground for a path or stepping stones, but all you see is fog and vines.

You take one tentative step forward.

"Not yet," calls a voice—actually, three voices in unison—from out of the mist. The voices echo all around you. Then they say, "Don't look at your feet."

Your head snaps up. Your body tenses. Your muscles tingle. Your eyes scan the landscape, trying to pierce the ever-thickening clouds. But you see nothing. You hear nothing. Until: "Now, step."

You do, almost as though you're being pulled along like a puppet. One foot steps into the mist, lands on something solid. Then, the other foot. And again, and again. Your head is held up high as if by a wire. Your eyes lock onto what's in front of you. Over and over, you remind yourself: Don't look down.

As your feet continue to travel of their own accord, as the landscape—an ongoing smear of gray fog and green vine—slowly rolls past, you realize gradually with a creeping suspicion that there are people stepping out of the mist and walking alongside you. You can't quite see them clearly, just glimmers and glances of purplish robes tinted green; tall, faded pyramidal hats; and pasty white skin.

And then your body stops moving, your head drops, your chin falls to your chest, and you see that you are once again on solid ground. When you look back up, you see that you're surrounded.

"Welcome to our coven, traveler," the mysterious beings all say in unison. Not a single mouth has moved, you realize, but the black eyes of the dozen or so beings gathered around you seem to grow wider with every word. "You are safe here—so long as you remain under our spell."

Turn to the Ordinary.

If you've watched *Star Wars: The Acolyte*, you know that the whole plot hinges on a misunderstanding. The Jedi and the coven of witches living on the planet Brendok don't bother trying to understand one another. They assume the worst in the other; they try to hold on to their own power; they believe that their interpretation of the Force is the right one. Conflict ensues. Lives are lost. Lies are told. And a legacy of deception unfolds. It's no wonder that twin sisters Osha and Mae turn to the dark side.

What goes wrong? The Jedi—in all their self-righteous, high-minded ideals—interrupt a ritual in which the two young girls are to become full-fledged members of the coven. The Jedi are concerned that the witches are abusing these children. And—not for nothing—the Jedi know that these girls are Force-sensitive; they might make good Jedi Knights one day. Consequently, they insist that the witches give these girls a choice: Stay with the coven or leave with the Jedi.

Lost on the Jedi, it seems, is the fact that they are also enlisting children into a spiritual tradition that these young minds can't yet fully understand. Rather than see this parallel as a source of common ground and an opportunity for collaboration, the Jedi and the witches fight over the destiny of these girls, with each side castigating the other.

Master Sol, a well-intentioned Jedi by all accounts, wants the best for the twins—at least, the best as he understands it to be. But tensions are high. Divided on whether to trust the Jedi, the witches unleash their magic in self-defense. Sol, believing that the twins' mother, Aniseya, is about to attack him, acts first. In the end, the entire coven is destroyed. Sol manages to save Osha but never tells the girl that he (accidentally) killed her mother. And the other Jedi? Well, they say nothing about the massacre on Brendok, which becomes a secret that literally kills them all.

But they were just trying to do the right thing, weren't they? At least, as they understood it. In the end, it didn't matter. It was the absence of any desire to truly understand those who were different that ultimately destroyed them all.

Christianity, like Islam and Buddhism, among others, is a missionary religion. This means that these religious traditions encourage believers to share their faith in the interest of spreading that faith by converting nonbelievers. A disordered missionary mindset can lead to war, violence, dehumanization, and perverted theology. If you believe you have exclusive possession of truth, then it's not a hard mental leap to look at others as less-than, inferior, and disposable. If you believe the truth that you possess *must* be accepted by everyone else at any cost, then it's again not a hard leap to justify violence, oppression, and tyranny. Obviously, this is a wrong kind of missionary mindset.

What if instead of bringing God to people near and far, we went in search of God at work already there? The Ignatian tradition insists that God is present in all things; it's foolish to think we might reach foreign shores before God does. Mission work, then, is less about *bringing* and more about *finding.*

I met Fr. Thomas Aquino Deshi Ramadhani, SJ, during a brief stay in Malindi, the coastal Kenyan town where he lived. Deshi is an Indonesian Jesuit who grew up in a religiously mixed household in which one parent was Muslim, the other Catholic. To the credit of his parents, this proved a spiritually rich environment in which their son came to deeply love, appreciate, and understand both his own Catholic faith and that of Islam.

It is not surprising that Deshi, a Catholic priest hailing from a predominantly Muslim country, was missioned to the majority Muslim community of Malindi for the purpose of establishing a ministry of interreligious dialogue. Interestingly, Deshi doesn't like that phrase. He prefers the term *inter-spiritual trialogue.*

Deshi is very aware of the temptation to debate, argue, and win even in the most well-intentioned of interreligious dialogues. After all, religion by any name brings with it a set of doctrines, norms, traditions, and rituals. But for Deshi, spirituality is something else, something bigger. Spirituality is the enjoying of God. Now this is something worth talking about! This is something that can be shared and savored without fear of condemnation or egotistical efforts to win a point. Reflecting on our own lived experiences, our own enjoyment of the Spirit, is indeed personal—that is, until we share it. We start with what we love, and because we love it, we *must* share it. And so we share it in love.

Recall that Deshi doesn't say inter-spiritual *dialogue*; rather, he says inter-spiritual *trialogue*. That small change in wording has a big effect: It makes room for God! A dialogue is between two people. But any talk of God should include God and make space for the Holy. Trialogue, then, is a conversation between me and you and the Divine. And whenever God enters the conversation, there's no need to win, no need to compete, no need to prove our point, let alone our worth. We show up on one another's shores not to convert but to treasure. To wonder. To delight and to share. To know one another better so as to come to know what God is already doing therein.

And now, cross the threshold that links the ordinary to the fantastical.

Everything about this moment stirs in you fear and anxiety. You are quite literally under the spell of strangers, whisked into a land of unknown dangers. It is a moment of profound discomfort.

And yet, you are safe, held tenderly in this web of magic. And the witches that stand around you—though unusual to your eye—are not threatening. Rather, they stand patiently waiting, curious.

You have a choice: Will you meet their gaze of curiosity, return wonder with awe? Or will you struggle against this mystery, these strangers? Your sword, after all, is not so far from your twitching fingers.

"I am looking for a wizard," you finally say. "I didn't mean to trespass but—"

The witches begin to whisper urgently, a sound that fills your ears like hissing steam. You take a step back, worried. Your fingers brush the hilt of your blade.

Then: "We know of the one you speak. We know this one as the Great Shaman. And yes, the Shaman has passed through our lands. The Shaman is a great friend of this coven." A beat, then: "And if you are a follower of the Shaman, then you are a friend of ours, too."

**At first, these witches evoke fear.
But what happens when we respond
instead with curiosity?**

THE TWENTY-FOURTH CONTEMPLATION

The Stars, or, The Vastness of Mystery

Step into adventure.

The sky feels very near in the marshlands. And big. The stunted trees, the murky waters, the encroaching shadows—the landscape feels small against the vastness of the void. You lie on a bed of moss, one hand tucked under your head, the other extended toward the starry heavens. You can barely even see your fingers in the darkness as they wiggle toward the stars.

The coven has lit a fire, but the purple-blue flames provide little light. The smoldering tongues are meant to keep unwanted predators from stumbling upon the resting witches—or so you've been told. You still haven't heard the sounds of any other living things. Even after a full day of travel through the marsh, you've seen no living thing other than the moss, the vines, and the shrubby trees.

Awash in the blanket of night, you find some peace. You listen to the soft breathing of the members of the coven. Scattered about the clearing, some are resting, some are asleep, and some are engaged in other nocturnal activities. Others gather around the fire sharing stories told in hushed whispers. And others—

Well, one of those others walks toward you now. Soft footfalls, the gentle rustle of flowing robes. Whoever it is, they stop just outside your peripheral vision, which registers a hooded figure silhouetted against the night sky.

"The stars are striking above the marshes, no?" the voice asks.

You mutter some affirmative response, shifting onto your side so as to face your conversation partner.

"No, no!" the witch says. "Keep gazing. I have not come to distract you from what the stars are saying. Only to sit and to listen with you."

"I'm not sure they're saying anything," you reply, rolling onto your back once more. "But they are beautiful. The view from here is just—well, I've never seen anything like it."

The witch says nothing at first. You steal a glance to make sure your companion hasn't left. But they remain just as they were, where they were.

"But what are they saying?" the witch whispers.

"Saying?"

"Perhaps it is different for you. But for us—the stars are whispers of a promise. A reminder that there is more. They are beacons from worlds that insist on existing. Isn't that the nature of light in darkness?"

* * *

Turn to the ordinary.

If we've learned anything from the voyages of the Starship Enterprise or any number of other *Star Trek* vessels, it's this: Space is the final frontier. We say that, of course, because space has no end. At least in the realm of *Star Trek*, because adventures go on and on not only through space but also through time, there is no shortage of mysteries to be explored.

How many of us gaze up at the stars with this mindset? Do we look into the vastness of space and allow our curiosity to be stoked? Do we question whether we are alone out here or whether there is more beyond what we can see? Do we wonder whether anyone is watching us? Of course, one overarching question concerns what we might learn from the planets, the moons, the stars. But perhaps even more important is the question of what they might teach us about ourselves. Because ultimately any venture out into God's creation is a venture inward, for we ourselves are vast just as space is vast, and God invites us to explore the mysteries of the fullness of ourselves just as God invites us out into the fullness of creation.

But do we look at our own lives with wonder and awe? Do we remember that we were created in the image and likeness of this same God of the Cosmos?

Jesuit brother and planetary scientist Guy Consolmagno offers a unique and helpful reading of the book of Job in his book *A Jesuit's Guide to the Stars: Exploring Wonder, Beauty, and Science.* Guy drops us into the final moments of Job's conversation with the Lord. This is a conversation born out of anger, frustration, and suffering on Job's part following the destruction of his family, livelihood, and lands. Job is at a loss to understand God's so-called plan and sees only chaos and sorrow. God does little to put Job's mind at ease. Instead, he throws big-picture questions at Job. "Where were you when I founded the earth?" God asks. "Into what were its pedestals sunk, and who laid its cornerstone, while the morning stars sang together and all the sons of God shouted for joy?"[50] Job is suffering, and God seems to be doing little more than offering an eclectic collection of riddles.

My take on God's response has always been one of frustrated acceptance. Job faces senseless suffering, suffering like what we see so often in our world. Our human minds can't make sense of it and so, turning to God, we ask, "Isn't there a plan?" God does not will suffering, and yet suffering exists. God is all-powerful and all-knowing, and since we are not, we throw up our hands and hope there's something more going on here, something beyond our ability to grasp. It's a rather unsatisfying answer.

But Br. Guy takes this exchange between Job and God someplace else entirely. Br. Guy isn't content with a God who toys with creation, who permits suffering and then waxes poetic about it. When God prompts Job with questions about the dwelling of light and the ordinances of heaven, it's not a test—it's an invitation. God isn't showing off; God is beckoning Job—and us, by extension—to discover the fullness of God's creation. "Come with God, and discover the way to the dwelling of light," Br. Guy writes. The message of Job becomes a hopeful one. For Br. Guy, who has made it his life's purpose to study the stars, this invitation was one he took up with excitement. God's invitation, though, is not only for planetary scientists and astronomers. "Anyone can take part in the game of being fascinated by the workings of the universe," Guy insists.[51]

I find this invitation compelling. As we gaze out into the wondrous expansiveness of God's great cosmos, it's easy to be overwhelmed. It's easy to assume our problems mean nothing and we are insignificant dust. In fact, such conclusions are not uncommon when dealing with the book of Job. Br. Guy disagrees. Look to the stars, he says. Recognize that God is calling us into something more. God is not content to leave us in ignorance; rather, God invites us into deeper knowing. This is how Br. Guy understands his vocations as a Jesuit and as a planetary scientist: "We get to play with [God], so to speak, uncovering the delightful puzzles he sets for us and marveling at the way the laws of the universe fit together with a logic that is both harmonious and elegant."[52] For Br. Guy, his work provides a glimpse into God's own personality.

I wonder, then, if, like the Magi following the star of Bethlehem, these distant glimmers of light are invitations to step beyond our knowing, beyond our comfort, into the vast mystery of God's own self. We seek after Christ who is pulsing in the very heart of creation and is found in surprising places, always calling to us. So, too, must we set aside our preconceptions. The Magi, after all, were not Jews; they came from distant lands with different customs. And yet they followed the star to Christ.

What stars are placed before us? In what ways do they beckon? What do they reveal about God's invitation? What light is this, and what does this light illuminate? What light is it calling forth from us?

Bernard of Clairvaux writes,

> O you, whoever you are, who feel that in the tidal wave of this world you are nearer to being tossed about among the squalls and gales than treading on dry land, if you do not want to founder in the tempest, do not avert your eyes from the brightness of this star. When the wind of temptation blows up within you, when you strike the rock of tribulation, gaze up at this star, call out to Mary. Whether you are being tossed about by the waves of pride or ambition or slander or jealousy, gaze up at this star, call out to Mary.[53]

We look up to the stars; we look up to Christ's own self. We set ourselves upon the path illuminated by Christ's light. We walk through wind and rain and we walk with our wounds and our sadness. We can do this because we walk by the light of the stars, trusting that within us Christ's own light burns brightly.

***

AND NOW, CROSS THE THRESHOLD THAT LINKS THE ORDINARY TO THE FANTASTICAL.

The witch, sitting silently in the lengthening shadow, has not said anything for some time. You continue staring at the stars but you catch yourself stealing sidelong glances toward your curious companion.

"Beacons?" you finally ask. "You believe the stars are beacons?"

"Beacons," comes the voice. "Yes. And what is the purpose of a beacon?"

"Uh—a beacon . . . it's a light."

"A beacon is a signal. A warning, perhaps. Or a guide. A beacon lights the way."

"Like a map?"

"Perhaps." The witch stands up, and you can just catch a twinkle in their eyes, a flash of white from their face. "Or, perhaps not. I can't help but think that a beacon invites a response, no? A course correction."

"They're just stars," you say. "Beautiful but—" You realize then that once more you are alone. And so you return to staring and wondering. And listening.

The stars call us out beyond ourselves. How do we respond to this invitation to seek after wonder and mystery?

THE TWENTY-FIFTH CONTEMPLATION

The Goddess Revealed, or, The Divine Reflection

Step into adventure.

You must have dozed off at some point because you realize that you're blinking your eyes awake. Something has pulled you from your slumber. But you can't quite dispel the fog of sleep. Or is that still just the mist from the marshlands? Either way, you push yourself up onto your elbows and squint against the darkness.

Except, it's not dark anymore. At least, not entirely. How long were you asleep?

A pinprick of light is casting its ray over the horizon, and you instinctively cover your eyes. But that's not quite right either. What you mistook for the light of the sun is instead a person dressed in a radiant white gown walking toward you. The person is barefoot, with long, loose brown hair. You can't make out the person's face just yet, but you feel something akin to kindness looking at you.

Not one of the witches, you decide. Not that they weren't kind, but the robes are all wrong. That's when you realize you're alone in the marsh; your companions have vanished. You feel oddly exposed.

Stumbling to your feet, you brush yourself off, scour the ground for your staff and it becomes clear to you that you're not in the marshland anymore either. You're in—well, you can't quite say. A meadow of yellow grain? A pasture with gently rolling hills? A valley from which you can somehow glimpse the ocean? Maybe a dream?

"Not a dream," the person says. She stands just in front of you now, smiling, arms at her side with hands outstretched as though to take yours. "Not quite."

The light is incredibly bright now.

"What, then?" you ask. "Am I dead?"

"From a certain point of view, yes. The better question is this one: Are you fully alive?"

"I don't understand," you mutter. "Where am I?"

The woman smiles, folding her hands and holding them at her chest. She gently bows her head. "I will see that you go where you are needed next," she said. "But try this question instead: What are you?"

It is then that you perceive that the source of the light is coming from behind your own eyelids.

Turn to the Ordinary.

The hero on an epic journey necessarily meets a goddess, or so the great mythologist Joseph Campbell tells us in his classic text *The Hero with a Thousand Faces*. The imagery is compelling, a scene taken right out of Nintendo's classic *The Legend of Zelda* games. Link, the series' protagonist, solves a puzzle and then—there she is! Squint your eyes just so, and even now you can almost see her materialize in a hodgepodge of blinking lights and fairy magic out of some mystical well.

For us in the Christian tradition, and for Catholics in particular, we have an easy and obvious corollary over which Nintendo has no copyright claim: Mary, the Mother of God, the God-Bearer, the Queen of Heaven. Mary is for us what Campbell claims is a necessary component in any heroic journey. And yet, I'm hesitant.

So much of Campbell's writing in this area feels uncomfortably gendered. A woman in myth means *this* and a man in myth means *that.* I am no mythologist, no Campbellian scholar, and so in my very nonacademic way, all I can say is that I don't care for it. This essentialism feels incomplete. Much of what Mary can teach us, I think, transcends gendered essentialism. After all, aren't we all called to be Bearers of Christ?

Even so, I think there is something useful for us here. I think we have in our own journeys an opportunity to approach the Blessed Mother with curiosity, with affection, with hope. Because while she is no goddess, she does show us the path to God in a way no one else can. "For she is the incarnation of the promise of perfection; the soul's assurance that, at the conclusion of its exile in a world of organized inadequacies, the bliss that once was known will be known again," Campbell writes of the so-called goddess and the role she can play in the sojourn of the hero.[54]

I'm struck by this. The goddess comes to us in our present place to remind us of what we had and can have again if we continue along the path. We often look to Mary as someone who embodies perfection—that perfect "yes" to God, as it were. And yet, Mary is so much more than this; she is more than any notion of perfection. In the Christian understanding, Mary was a human just like any of us, and she had her own joys and sorrows, challenges and surprises. She walked the path of mortality just as we do. Obsessing over her perfection can rob her of her humanness and, I think, what she wishes to reveal to us: We, too, are human. We, too, are given opportunities to fully embody God, to welcome God's Spirit into our very selves, to be Christ-bearers to the world. The "goddess" of our story desires to hold up a mirror so that we can see the same image of divinity sparkling in our very selves.

And that brings me to another line from Campbell I find helpful: "She can never be greater than [the hero], though she can always promise more than [the hero] is yet capable of comprehending."[55]

Let's discard any Campbellian impulse to limit or reduce women and instead let's turn to Mary's own words: "God has looked upon his handmaid's lowliness; behold, from now on will all ages call me blessed."[56] Our meeting with a "goddess" is a reminder that God deals intimately and directly with those who are most vulnerable, those who are forgotten or cast aside. Indeed, Mary would not call herself "greater" even when she was carrying the Christ. And yet, the downward mobility to which Christ invites us—a rejection of riches, honors, and pride—is the very path upon which we experience God's grace, the path that redeems the world God still imagines. Here, along this path, in the company of this very human woman born into a very particular time and place and from a very particular socioeconomic category, we find perfection. Perhaps there is hope for us, then, too!

Even this, Mary transcends. The Catholic Church recognizes countless apparitions (mystical appearances) of the Blessed Mother the world over. She comes to communities big and small, well-known and well off the beaten path, to bring a word of comfort or of warning, and always to bring the Gospel. She appears as part of the community—her skin, her hair, her clothes mirroring local customs—thereby reminding each person she meets that they, too, are blessed. They, too, are God's chosen people in all their unique specificity.

I am drawn to the image of Mary as the moon to God's bright sun. Mary reflects that holy light in the same way the moon reflects the sun's light. But more than that, Mary reflects the light of God in us. Mary holds up a mirror and invites us to gaze upon ourselves, fellow Christ-bearers, beacons of God's glory. Mary's story is one of pilgrimage, of carrying Christ and going to where Christ is needed; Mary is always comforting Jesus's friends and the people of God. But Mary invites us along that road, too. Mary challenges us to see in our own vocation that same invitation to pilgrimage. In accepting that invitation, we accept the promise of the goddess that assures us of our own unique vocations that is always expanding.

* * *

AND NOW, CROSS THE THRESHOLD THAT LINKS THE ORDINARY TO THE FANTASTICAL.

"I am the Lady of Moon and Mist," the woman says. "I come to you now to bring you where you need next go. But first, you must look inside yourself. You saw the stars, I know, and were enchanted by their number. But do you not see that same vastness within your own soul? That same glorious light radiating out?"

You touch your hand to your chest, feeling the warmth of the light. You've felt this way before; others have been that warmth, that light. But now you wonder: Can you share this same feeling with those in need? Can you offer that same comfort?

You stare into this strange woman's eyes, searching. But she says nothing more, simply stares back. And the more she looks at you, the more you see yourself. But not just yourself—others, too. Because what she's said about you and your light isn't just true of you; it's true of everyone.

She reaches out, takes your hand, and the world changes again.

The goddess extends a promise of future glory. What holds us back from embracing and sharing that gift?

THE TWENTY-SIXTH CONTEMPLATION

The Unicorn, or, The Glimmer of Hope

Step into adventure.

On the other side of things stands a unicorn. There, in the shadow of a great keep—which itself sits in the shadow of a great mountain—stands a humble, marvelous unicorn. And it's grazing.

Or, it was, before you stumbled into the meadow and disturbed the peace and quiet and the gently resting fireflies that are—against all laws of nature—glowing even now, even in the middle of the day. The meadow is expansive. Tall grasses wave a welcome in the gentle wind.

And the unicorn—well, the unicorn stands at attention. Its eyes meet your own. Its mouth continues to slowly chew the glistening green grass, but those eyes are studying you. And so you study the creature in return.

What do you see?

A magnificent white horse with a mane of every color you've ever been able to put a name to and many you still cannot. Protruding from its head is a horn the color of cream but also the color of magic and of destiny and of hope. Its hooves seem to glisten with sparkling dust and as it moves, the dust falls upon the grass, and each tiny blade grows an inch taller.

"You're beautiful," you say. The words escape of their own accord, but they feel right and natural. It's the only way to respond to this sense of peace that has rested upon you. Consolation. Hope. Staring at the unicorn standing within its aura of magic has calmed your soul and lifted your gaze.

Everything feels possible now. Everything feels just as it should be. You are ready to carry on or stay put, whatever the moment requires.

* * *

TURN TO THE ORDINARY.

As it turned out, the Renaissance Faire was the unicorn's side hustle. Professionally, the little creature was a caregiver, visiting hospitals where sick kids needed a touch of magic, a whisper of hope.

I learned all this as we waited in line to visit the magical horse. My girls, decked out head to toe in princess gear, were waiting for their chance to pet a real live unicorn. Then there was the whole unicorn-magic-dust-wish grand finale, which we were all pretty excited about. Pet the unicorn, snap a photo, get dust sprinkled on your head, and make a wish. Not a bad day.

"It's just a little horse with a horn," my brother said. He was worried the girls would see through the illusion. But they didn't. All they saw was a unicorn arrayed in magic, and it was standing right before them.

I wondered if that's what those kids in the hospitals saw, too. I mean, we all saw that horse with the horn; it's not hard to reduce that which stands before us to the simple facts of life. Those kids in those hospitals: *I'm sick; I'm dying. Chances are this; my prognosis is that.* But when we see a unicorn instead of a horse with a horn, I wonder if our horizons don't lift. Those hard facts of life get blessed with a touch of enchantment. Perhaps there's more here than meets the eye. Perhaps the mystery of life is more than the sum of its parts. Perhaps a bit of imagination, a bit of dreaming, and a polished horn can transform this humble animal into a creature of myth and wonder.

And perhaps my disease can be transformed, too. Perhaps my suffering, my sadness, the hole in my chest and the losses I've had to bear. Perhaps hope remains when I allow something mysterious to break through and bind up all these hard facts of life into a beautiful, heartbreaking story.

"And hope does not disappoint," St. Paul tells the Romans. But hope is not some parent rushing out to fulfill birthday promises. Hope is not a magician or a genie or a magic spell. Hope is a way of looking at things, an audacious claim that *yes, even here, even now* something good can come. Hope is our gaze falling upon the magic and the wonder amidst the pain and the suffering. Hope is our insistent call to look beyond the raw facts of the day to see the Great Storyteller drawing us near. Hope is the willingness to embrace consolation and possibility even when everything screams to the contrary.

But hope, too, is work. Hope is not passive. Once our eyes fall upon that Source of Consolation, once God touches our very soul with that enchanting grace, we then get up and make ourselves available to the possibility of the miraculous. Hope is making room for the miraculous. Hope is the space we give to God to work through us in small and tremendous ways. Hope is our embrace of the truth that the story is not yet done, and neither are we.

AND NOW, CROSS THE THRESHOLD THAT LINKS THE ORDINARY TO THE FANTASTICAL.

The unicorn marches over to where you stand—a regal, powerful strut—and nuzzles your hand. Your fingers tingle at the touch. The sensation travels down your arm and rests in your soul. You can feel your whole body glow.

You look up at the castle before you and the mountains beyond. Shadows are here, cast upon the very ground on which you stand. But with this blessed creature, in this moment of bliss, you feel nourished. Warm. Ready. And you wonder: Can the shadow ever truly fall upon a creature as radiant as this? Now that you've touched it, bonded with it, you ask a different question: Can the shadow ever truly fall upon you?

When a common beast of burden dons a simple horn, it becomes something hopeful and lovely. How does the sight of a unicorn invite us to reassemble the hard facts of our lives?

THE TWENTY-SEVENTH CONTEMPLATION

The Knight, or, The Dualistic Trap

STEP INTO ADVENTURE.

You are loath to turn toward the sound of hurried hooves. You'd rather dwell in the moment's peace. You want to bask in the sun's rays and watch as the light, refracted off the unicorn's horn, dances upon the grass. Gazing upon this majestic creature and standing in its calming presence . . . well, it's a feeling you can't quite put words to. It's certainly one you don't want to see come to an end.

"You, there!" The voice rises to a volume that can be heard above the clamor of the approaching stampede. You purse your lips and tighten your grip on your staff. "Stop where you are!"

You turn slowly, determined to prove that you are no threat. But the horsemen—there are thirteen of them—barrel down upon you, encircling you in two concentric circles. The horses slow to a trot. Their riders point their weapons—spears and short swords—at your head.

"Friend or foe?" This from the man you presume to be in command. He sits atop his white steed, covered in polished metal and decorative banners. His horse stands directly in front of you. His voice—a tinny sound—comes from within his horned helmet.

"To whom?" you ask. You lean on your staff and stare.

"Friend or foe?" the knight asks again. "It is a simple question."

"I like to think I'm friend to all and foe to none," you say with a shrug. "But I'm not at all sure who you are, and I certainly don't know who you're talking about so . . ."

The knight leaps from his horse, landing on the ground with a thud. He draws his sword and points it at your chest. "A jester, then," he says. "A purveyor of frivolous words and meaningless acts." You can feel the tip of the sword press against your sternum. "We are a people at war," the knight continues. "We protect our friends and vanquish our foes. We do not appreciate those who would trespass on our lands. So let me make this quite simple for you, Jester: Are you good? Or are you bad? Are you one of us? Or do I need to slay you where you stand?"

Turn to the Ordinary.

Chivalric. Valliant. Brave. Virtuous. Gallant. Knightly.

These words are all basically synonyms. To be a knight, both historically and in the stereotypical fantasy story, is to manifest these high and holy attributes. Or at least to pretend to. What pressure! To be all these things all the time feels unrealistic at best; at worst, grating on your very self. Who can hit such a high mark all the time? We all have flaws. None of us is perfect. And yet, we pretend that a knight is, simply by definition!

It's no wonder that storytellers from Geoffrey Chaucer to Monty Python have had their share of fun playing with this heroic caricature. We readers love chuckling at the shortcomings of these supposedly unbreakable men. (And they are all men, aren't they? A dualistic trap.) When we catch a glimpse of what's going on behind the curtain, we realize that knights are people just like us, muddling through life, struggling to figure out the next right thing. Perhaps we see our own journeys reflected in their efforts. We see our own aspirations.

But the mythos of a knight is not that of a fallible man, as someone prone to shortcomings. No—the knight must be *more*, must be *better.* He must embody the code of perfection. After all, why bother idolizing someone who's no better than you are?

And so the knight who represents all that is good necessarily must clash in battle against all that is bad. The knight, to put it another way, embodies a dualistic view of the world. It's easier that way, right? Anoint the good guy; chase down and slay the bad guy. Avoid the nuanced lands of gray where we typically spend our time. Would that our lives were so simple!

But, over and over again, what we see in stories of knights is that this dichotomy cannot hold. When we put someone on a pedestal and hold them to the standard of perfection, we can only look forward to disappointment. And when that disappointment arrives, when we realize that perfection is always just beyond our grasp, we turn to violence. Realizing that he's fallen short of his expected role, our stalwart knight unsheathes the blade and points it at a supposed enemy. Because even if he can't fully embody the heavy burden of perfection, at least he can imitate the good guy in his efforts to name (and destroy) something (or someone) supposedly bad.

In these ways, we erect the scaffolding of a dualistic worldview: good or bad, man or woman, strong or weak, rich or poor, and so on. Then we insist on protecting that worldview. We insist on conducting our lives as if they aren't muddled by choices that refuse such clean distinction. We avoid the possibility that there might be multiple good choices. And we do all we can to prevent ourselves from seeing the world from someone else's point of view, lest our own be challenged and crumble. Our proverbial knight winds up guarding this decaying worldview rather than promoting and protecting the good of all people. He stands as a bastion against forces that have already overtaken the land.

We need to begin our spiritual journeys with a sense of right and wrong, good and bad. This dualistic way of proceeding is helpful in the opening chapters of our stories. But we cannot remain there. We cannot separate our lives or our world into *good* and *bad*. Instead, we are called by God to seek out the good anywhere and everywhere. God doesn't set a bar and then expect us to leap over it to achieve goodness; this is the wrong way to visualize the challenge. Instead, God proclaims that goodness is inherent in who and what we already are, which means that goodness is everywhere, in everyone, and finding it does not involve jumping through hoops.

What if we set aside our need to be right, or on the right side, and instead simply make up our minds to stand with others to see what they see, and maybe even marvel at how and why they see it? When we break free of this dualism, we realize we don't need a good guy and a bad guy to wage war against one another. We can rewrite the plot. We can recast our expectations. We do that by falling into the embrace of our loving God who calls *all* things good, and who asks us to go out into the whole of creation and find and celebrate those many good things.

And now, cross the threshold that links the ordinary and fantastical.

You stand your ground, staring into the eye-sockets of the knight's helmet.

"I am a friend," you say. "I wonder why I've been greeted as an enemy."

The knight lowers the blade, returning it to his sheath. He raises a hand and the other riders lower their weapons as well. "One cannot be too cautious during a time of war."

"War?" you ask. "I see no war. Just beauty and—"

"It's all around you," the knight fires back. "Those of us sworn to protect the greater good can never tire of chasing down those who would destroy it."

"Sounds exhausting," you say with a grin.

"And you sound like a spy."

You shake your head. "I, too, am a friend of the greater good," you say.

"Then you will prove it," the knight replies. "In these lands, there are two types of creatures: the virtuous and the vile. You have already seen the former. Now, I ask you to rid us of the latter."

"You want me to go find every—"

"No," the knight cuts in. "I want you to prove that you can destroy that which is evil. There is a dragon in those mountains," he says, gesturing to the towering peaks in the near distance. "It brings nothing but death and sorrow with every flap of its vile wings. You say you're a friend of the greater good? Then you'll have no trouble ridding our lands of this villain."

You incline your head slightly, though your thoughts are troubled. Surely, there is another way?

The knight insists we wage war against an enemy. But what happens when instead we recognize our common humanity, our shared Creator?

THE TWENTY-EIGHTH CONTEMPLATION

The Dragon, or, Befriending Our Inner Beast

Step into adventure.

The dragon's lair is high up in the mountains. It takes the better part of the day to reach it. You're tired now, sweaty and worn out. You pause to look back over the way you've come: the slow and steady incline through the mountain pass, riddled with tiny, loose stones and sharp, protruding rocks. It has not been an easy climb. There's a thin line of blood on your hands from a gash that refuses to close.

Beyond the mountain pass lies the castle, dark and foreboding, and the whole of the meadow. It looks peaceful. It was peaceful. But now your attention must turn to violence, to where peace is absent. You give the meadow your back and continue trudging across the barren terrain.

When you come upon the dragon, you gasp. The creature is tremendous: a purplish black beast, all scales and claws and torn wings. It's asleep, nestled in a crevice along the mountainside directly beneath you. You can feel the stones rumble with each heavy breath.

You creep toward it slowly, quietly, silently drawing your sword. You're standing directly above the great beast with your blade angled at its exposed neck. It looks harmless from here, just another animal at rest. But you know that can't be true. You try to call to mind all the harm this creature has undoubtedly done, all the lives it has ruined.

The blade trembles in your hand. The stories you want to tell yourself about this beast simply don't line up with the truth of the sleeping creature beneath you.

Well—that is, until it wakes up. Until your chance at a quick victory is dashed upon the hardened rock of the mountains around you. The dragon yawns, its eyes flickering awake and glaring at you. Its great head rises up, and you adjust your blade's angle to account for this unhappy turn of events.

Now you'll see which version of the beast is easier to kill: The sleeping unknown or the roaring reality.

Turn to the ordinary.

In the opening pages of his dark fairy tale, *Coraline*, Neil Gaiman paraphrases G. K. Chesterton: "Fairy tales are more than true not because they tell us dragons exist but because they tell us dragons can be defeated."[57]

I've always loved this quasi-mantra. The idea therein threads the needle between fantasy and reality, highlighting the interplay between what we know to be true and what we feel might yet be. I was so taken by this quote, in fact, that I decided I wanted to emblazon the words upon the walls of the nursery of our firstborn daughter. I hoped that she'd be just as inspired by this fairy tale lesson as I—at least, once she was old enough to read. And so, in the months before our daughter's arrival, I combed through the internet trying to find some illustrated version of the quote that would bring this interplay between the spiritual and the fantastical to life.

The quote was easy; I can type and cite with the best of them, and I'm not completely incompetent when it comes to Adobe Photoshop. But what image would I pair with the words? What would enchant the eye of my baby girl as she grew and learned and wondered? I was searching for something epic. But I encountered a problem: This quote, and my subsequent internet searches, tended to attract one bloody, violent image after the next. A girl rushing into battle with a fire-breathing monster. A girl holding high a severed head. A girl thrusting the tip of her blade into the belly of a giant beast. Not quite the vibe for a nursery. Violence, bloodshed, battle—this wasn't the raw material of fantasy and dreams that I hoped to offer my children. In fact, it was just the opposite.

I fine-tuned my search parameters. *Girl and dragon.* A new genre of image appeared: A girl serenely sitting beside a dragon. A young girl gently patting the head of a monster. A small girl sharing a cup of tea with a great scaly beast. Now we were getting somewhere! Friendship! Peace! Acceptance! Curiosity! These were the kinds of things I wanted my daughter to see. The dragon didn't need to be dead; it didn't even need to be on the attack.

Something else soon became clear: I don't actually want to teach my children to wage war against the many inevitable dragons in their lives. I want them to *befriend* their dragons. I want them to make peace with them, to offer an olive branch of mercy to them, and gain understanding of themselves by nurturing curiosity and wonder toward these uncomfortable parts of life. Because, as the fantastical mantra that set me upon this quest in the first place makes clear, dragons aren't *really* real. We rarely come face-to-face with great fire-breathing monsters. But we do pull our hair out with anxiety and worry and fear and shame and despair and sorrow. These imaginary dragons cause us very real harm.

How easy it is to fight and to hate these sorts of dragons! How easy it is to turn our proverbial swords upon our own selves. How easy it is to become obsessed with our so-called shortcomings, those untidy parts of ourselves that give us headaches and make us feel less-than. But when we lob off the head of anxiety, or fear, or fill-in-the-blank, three more heads sprout up to take its place.

I've heard far too many spiritually minded people claim we need to wage spiritual warfare against those parts of ourselves that we dislike or that cause us pain. We need to drive out fear, anxiety, and shame. But I'm of the mind that such self-inflicted violence leads nowhere, and that in fact we cannot drive these supposed "bad" parts away.

We spend so much time thinking we need to wage war against these dragons when the better way to approach them is with a desire to understand and embrace them, and realize they're part of the adventure, part of the journey, part of the world in which God has turned us loose to live our lives. Instead of plunging our blade into their gut, we might instead offer our dragons a cup of tea. We might sit alongside them, pet their tails, and talk things over.

This is the artwork I'd like to hang on my daughter's bedroom wall. Perhaps it's the artwork we should hang in our hearts.

"We don't make progress when we demonize," writes Fr. Greg Boyle. "We should abandon that altogether, and in all circumstances refuse to do it"—including, I would add, when we look at our own selves. Instead, Fr. Boyle insists that we must see ourselves and others as wounded and in need of healing rather than either good or evil. When we change the paradigm, both the problem and the solution change, too. A wounded person needs to be made whole, not locked away or destroyed. That changed paradigm doesn't alter the fact that something unfortunate or possibly even tragic has taken place. Still, Fr. Boyle boldly declares that we are all unshakably good. "Surely, we can hold something as horrible and still not make monsters of anyone," Fr. Boyle says. "Demonizing keeps us from solutions. Plus, it's always the opposite of how God sees."[58] That's a powerful reminder to look at ourselves—even at our own dragons—as God does: with love, mercy, and delight.

* * *

And now, cross the threshold that links the ordinary to the fantastical.

You stand stock-still, sword at the ready, staring into the dragon's eyes. You're sure it's about to strike: some combination of a fireball and poison bite. But it doesn't.

Somehow, it seems to know that you've stayed your blade. Somehow, it seems to see within you the uncertainty laced with compassion. Somehow, this great beast that you thought was nothing but violence and death is grateful to you for pausing and wondering instead of plunging that deadly sword into its sleeping belly.

You lower your blade, and the dragon lowers its head, coming just within reach. You feel hot air blasting from its wrinkled nostrils. You can see yourself reflected in its great black eyes. And you wonder—you wonder! You wonder about its scales and its lifespan and its family and its kind. You allow your curiosity to overtake you and reach out a hand to touch one of those rough scales.

Another blast of hot air. The creature is still an animal, still a powerful, hungry being made of flame and claws. But it's not evil. It's not bad. And you find yourself smiling because if this monstrous creature can be more than—or is it other than?—bad, then there's hope for all creatures everywhere.

Dragons exist not to embody evil but to remind us that even the most frightening creature is a creature of God. How does such a reminder demand we look anew at our world and ourselves?

THE TWENTY-NINTH CONTEMPLATION

The Battle, or, The Discomfort We Have with Peace

Step into adventure.

The sheer magnitude of the violence is overwhelming.

As you stumble down the mountainside, you see it: War. You hear it, too, the clashing armor and ringing steel and the final grunts of dying soldiers. The meadow that was recently so peaceful has erupted in flame and blood and fear. Knights on horseback plunge into crashing waves of twisted, dark creatures. You can see from your great height as one knight's spear plunges into the gut of a goblin. Another lops off the head of a humanoid creature with fangs and curved horns.

You have no idea what these things are or where they came from. You barely have time to think about what they might be trying to accomplish. Storm the castle? Burn the meadow? Simply kill and loot and rampage? You've never seen such destruction.

You realize that you've stopped running, that you're frozen in place, staring. You blink twice, urging your body to move, your legs to pump, your lungs to suck in the needed air. And you wonder, What can I contribute? What am I called to do in this moment?

"You've not come this far for slaughter," your spirit guide whispers.

"But I'm here all the same," you reply. "I have to do something." You pull your sword from its sheath as you break into a sprint.

"All the same: You've not come this far for slaughter."

You grit your teeth and try to chase the voice from your head. You're here and you're needed and you're going to do your best.

You adjust the weapon in your hand and keep running.

* * *

Turn to the ordinary.

We turn to violence when we believe all other options have been exhausted. We respond in self-defense when we are attacked. We stand up to the bully on behalf of the vulnerable—on the playground, the city street, or the global stage. We calculate the needs of the greater good and decide that there is no other choice. Often, violence seems to be the necessary response—even when we prefer to do no harm.

In the global arena, we use the theory of just war to rationalize our actions and guide our decisions. Have we exhausted all other options? Are we responding in a way that is proportional? Is there a reasonable belief that this act of violence will achieve the good end for which we hope? Who defines "the good?" We do what we can to mitigate the inevitable suffering and death that will unfold. We know we live in a broken world, we reason; what else can we do but play the hand we're dealt?

This is not the place to debate just war theory, though it is worth noting that Pope Leo XIV considers it outdated. But it is a place to remind ourselves that within the Catholic tradition, we also have what is called *just peace*. Why does this matter? Because a framing of just peace rather than just war flips the paradigm. When trying to justify violence we ultimately find ourselves running through a checklist. If we check enough boxes, then we respond. And if we respond, we likely do so in a way that leaves us feeling uncomfortable. After all, we were made for community; we were not made to destroy one another. But with a paradigm of just peace, we abandon the checklists. We no longer play the role of beleaguered judge; we become an active contributor promoting a *good* rather than mitigating a *bad*.

There are three "streams" of just peace that scholars invite us to consider.[59] The first, a series of just peace principles, is inspired by the work of Maryann Cusimano Love and can be used to guide our action. These principles include *just cause* (the protecting, defending, and restoring of human dignity); *right relationships* (the creation of relationships that are just and lasting); and *reconciliation* (a prioritization of the healing of wounds). There are more, but you can already see how these principles invite us into meaningful encounters that should be cultivated at all times.

The second stream, derived from the work done by ethicist Glen Stassen and theologian Susan Brooks Thistlethwaite, proposes just peace norms. These norms invite us to move from limiting the violence of war to promoting and practicing the life-giving work of peace. Again, we see the opportunity to act *for* a good rather than *against* a bad.

The third stream, which builds upon the first two, proposes just peace virtue ethics. Virtues, Catholic peace activist and poet Rose Marie Berger writes, cultivate a disposition to do the good. Such inner work allows us to build a firm spiritual foundation from which we see past simply "doing the good" and instead react instinctively to meet injustice and violence with a desire for generativity and full human flourishing. Catholic theological virtue ethicist Eli S. McCarthy offers a core question to help focus the work of a just peace virtue ethics: "What kind of people are we becoming?"[60] Again, we see the emphasis not on solely mitigating my less-than-good actions but on building up something that is truly good for the whole of creation.

Ultimately, just peace is about building something new. Just peace is about sustaining and nurturing relationships that withstand the temptation to violence. Just peace reorients our horizon toward what is needed for everyone to flourish, rather than limiting us to what should be avoided in order to merely exist. Let us then cultivate in ourselves a desire to work for peace. Let us do the daily work of building up communities that are just and compassionate, that nurture loving-kindness and strengthen bonds among strangers. Let us lean into the creative tension that striving for peace in a world marred by violence demands.

AND NOW, CROSS THE THRESHOLD THAT LINKS THE ORDINARY TO THE FANTASTICAL.

You rush into battle with little thought to how ill-prepared you are. You have no training; you have no experience. You have a sword that you've barely swung and a stick that's better used for walking. But you see no other option—you have to do something.

"You've not come this far for slaughter." The spirit guide again. You try to silence the voice but when you do, all you hear are the screams of battle. The screams of slaughter.

Is there another way? Or is it all too far gone? Even here, even now, you wonder. Even here, even now, you turn to curiosity. What does the moment demand?

**The great battle seems inevitable.
And yet, what if even now, even in this moment,
we ask ourselves what peace might look like,
what different sort of world a disposition built
on peace might envision?**

THE THIRTIETH CONTEMPLATION

The Orc, or, What to Do with the Unredeemable

STEP INTO ADVENTURE.

At the end of your blade is a sniveling, pathetic creature. Snot drips from its flattened nose and its body is caked in grime and grease. It sneers at you with a mouth full of crooked, dirty teeth. Or—you realize—not teeth per se but just gums that are bleeding black. It's not a pretty sight.

What is this thing that has caused so much suffering? An orc? A goblin? Some other creature of ash and shadow? It has dogged you in your journey, this thing. It has clung to you in your dreams, weighed you down in body and mind. It has haunted you and hunted you. And why should it? Look at it—it's weak, craven, dead-eyed, and soulless. It has no power, not by itself. There, on its knees, it trembles and licks its lips, some misshapen animal.

This creature is in your power now, and it will get what it deserves, what it's given you: a taste of chaos, of hell itself.

"Do it," the thing snickers. "Or are you too much of a coward?"

Still licking its lips, its eyes dart all over the place with no discernible purpose.

You pause. Your arm remains straight and strong, your blade leveled at the thing's neck. It would be justice, no? A swift end would be better than what this thing has dealt to so many. One sure strike—that's better than the lingering terror this creature has inflicted.

And yet you hesitate. You search its uncanny eyes, uncomfortable with the conclusions you've stumbled upon. You shift your stance, feeling the firmness of the stone beneath you. You wish your own resolve were as solid, that there were no question what must be done now, with this captive in your grasp.

"Do it," the thing says again, like a smear on your honor. You grit your teeth, never letting your gaze or your blade fall.

TURN TO THE ORDINARY.

There is an insight from a podcast I heard several years ago that I return to quite frequently. This was a political podcast, and the guest was offering analysis into the political climate of polarization and distrust.

There's so much anger and division, the guest noted. Which was true enough then and still is, as of this writing. But anger and division are not inherently bad things, the guest contended. In fact, in politics, this guest continued, we take stands for and argue over things we believe in. We naturally get angry; we naturally take sides. This is fine. The problem, the guest said, is when we turn not to anger and division but to contempt and dismissal. This, I learned, is the poison pill of countless relationships. The movement from passionate anger to apathetic dismissal is a death knell.

How often do we make this turn in our relationships, whether personal, professional, or communal? How often do we decide our opposition is no longer worth debating in good faith, and our opponents should be dismissed and forgotten? When we turn to contempt and dismissal, we make a spiritual claim about our opponent: *Not only does my opponent have no value; my opponent is beyond the hope of redemption.* That, of course, is a claim that is anathema to the Christian worldview, which holds that everything and everyone is redeemable; nothing and no one is beyond redemption.

In stories, orcs are typically relegated to the category of "beyond redemption." They are disposable, fallen, beyond the pale. They are the foot soldiers of dark powers and they must be defeated if the powers of darkness are to be pushed back. But I wonder, is that the worldview we desire? Is that sniveling creature at the end of our blade not worth an ounce of compassion, pity, or mercy?

Are these orcs we see thrashing about the world in fact reflections of ourselves? We, too, can spend far too much time worrying over whether we're redeemable, lovable, worthy of anyone's attention. We, too, often feel like sniveling, grimy, worthless beings. We know what it's like to be flailing about in our daily lives, and we know what we need in response: an outstretched hand rather than the sharp end of a sword.

What is that part of ourselves that we would rather kill than redeem? Our fear? Anxiety? Lust or gluttony? What is it about our own beings that feel orc-ish? Do we see parts of ourselves as deserving of nothing more than a blade to the gut? What if instead we threw our arms around those troublesome traits in love and mercy? What if we showed our own orc-ish selves a bit of forgiveness rather than contempt and dismissal?

Here's the important truth: Either we're all redeemable, or we're all expendable. Does that change how you see the orcs in your life? The neighbor whose ideology offends you and the politician who stands for everything you despise and the family member who continues to wreak havoc on your mental psyche. Stand up for truth and justice, push back against false narratives and hate, and protect yourself and others. But remember this: No one is beyond redemption. Those proverbial orcs share our same humanity.

"It's a pity Bilbo didn't kill Gollum when he had the chance," a beleaguered Frodo Baggins says to the wizard Gandalf in *The Fellowship of the Ring.* Frodo knows that having the creeping, crawling, tenacious once-hobbit on their trail will lead to problems. Frodo knows, too, that his uncle, Bilbo Baggins, had the chance to end Gollum's life and chose instead to leave the creature alive and at large. Frodo, sitting in his own darkness and worry, can hardly see the value of such a decision.

"Pity?" Gandalf echoes. "It was Pity that stayed [Bilbo's] hand. . . . Do not be too eager to deal out death in judgement. For even the very wise cannot see all ends."[61] Gandalf believes Gollum has a part to play in the story—and indeed, he does. Without Gollum, the ring would never have been destroyed; light would not have triumphed over darkness.

Curiosity leads us to wonder about the possibilities still hidden within even the most orcish of people. Curiosity makes room for the seemingly impossible. The pity of Bilbo was perhaps less a kindness than it was a chance for something different, something more. Where there is life, there is hope. Bilbo recognized that he could not see the end of all things and so resisted the temptation to end even one life.

AND NOW, CROSS THE THRESHOLD THAT LINKS THE ORDINARY TO THE FANTASTICAL.

Slowly, you lower your blade. Your face remains set, the corners of your lips tight. But you gesture ever so slightly to the hideous creature in front of you. "Go."

It laughs, a cruel, haunting sound. "You'll regret it," it hisses.

"Maybe," you say. But at least you won't regret having killed the thing. And with life comes hope, and possibility. Perhaps you won't live to regret your decision. Perhaps you'll live to celebrate it.

All the same, you watch the creature lope away into the darkness. But just before it vanishes, you catch it looking back over its shoulder one final time. There's a look in its face you can't read. In response, you simply hold its gaze.

It sneers at you and disappears into the shadows. And you turn and carry on. For some reason, you feel a bit lighter.

The orc confronts us with an uncomfortable truth: We must always leave room for redemption. But do we truly believe that every person is redeemable?

THE THIRTY-FIRST CONTEMPLATION

The Castle, or, Where the Power Really Lies

STEP INTO ADVENTURE.

You find yourself on horseback racing across the bloodied, beaten landscape. Hand-to-hand combat rages on every side, with the sounds of shouts and cries and jeers and clashing swords ringing out. Clouds gather overhead. The light upon the land dims—an ominous sign.

But you ride on, your countenance set, your gaze cast upon the looming castle on the horizon. The horse—you don't know its name, you're not even sure where it has come from—is strong and sturdy. You can feel the creature's muscles working, pumping. You're grateful for the beast. You're grateful for its speed and agility. With each thumpa-pump-pump of its pounding hooves, the immediate danger recedes further into the background. Even so, you remain haunted by the death and destruction and the anger and the hate. It must come to an end. Lives cannot be so casually tossed aside. You ride on because you are certain that within those castle walls lie the answers you seek to the riddle of peace in this ravaged land.

Or, at the very least, you believe that within that towering monument to temporal power lies one who can grapple with those riddles. Someone who can dictate terms of peace and prosperity, who needs but a little nudge to get off the sidelines and into the fray. Why else build a castle if not to showcase a willingness to protect?

You're within the city walls now. You're one lone rider bearing a banner of hope. Who would bother to stop you? And so you persist, picking your way across empty streets and under ancient causeways and up winding paths until you stand at the castle's great gate. You dismount. With war on your mind but peace in your heart, you put a hand on the keep's door and push.

* * *

Turn to the ordinary.

"Destroy this temple, and in three days I will raise it up," Jesus says. The Jews looked at each other and shrugged, probably thinking something along the lines of *This guy—am I right?!?* But they replied, "'This temple has been under construction for forty-six years, and you will raise it up in three days?' But he was speaking about the temple of his body."[62]

I like this little back and forth. From the vantage point of some two thousand-plus years, we look at this scene and smile. *How quaint,* we think. *They didn't realize he meant the story of Easter.* I mean, Jesus was a carpenter and a miracle worker, but even he was like, *Yeah, obviously I don't mean this literally. I'm talking about rising from the dead, folks, not hiring a time traveling construction crew.*

We laugh, perhaps, but this scene remains vitally instructive. Again and again, Jesus reminds us that it's not the physical building that is important; it's not the *human made constructs* that hold the keys. It's God's own Holy Spirit; it's Christ alive within us and glimmering in all of creation. We get so distracted by temporal power, by immense buildings and by convoluted dogma, that at times we forget it's all pointing beyond itself. The temple, after all, is only as useful as it is successful at getting people closer to God. Same goes for our churches and synagogues and mosques and holy places. The same goes, in fact, for our religions and our rituals. There is so much good and beauty therein and yet these things are only the gateway. We must pass through and pass over into the dream to which God beckons us. We must do so *together.*

It's too easy to focus solely on maintaining the structures of our faith—the literal churches and the theological teachings. These are important, of course, but if our attention remains only on these temporal things, we may risk missing the God to whom they point. We pull our hair out because the temple is crumbling, and yet we miss the Risen Lord standing in the rubble.

So, too, in our temporal affairs. We look to the wielders of power, forgetting that we ourselves have much to give. We wring our hands, hoping that structures of society hold, while forgetting that it is within our ability to build something new, now.

Because here's the thing: Christ is just as present in each of us as he is in any church. Let us not look to these buildings as keepers of the Christlight; let us look to them as mirrors that reflect the Christlight radiating from within our souls. Let us look to them not as places to gather but as the means to gather by, the call that we each hear and respond to, the foundation not of brick and mortar but of community and kinship. And then let us walk confidently into a world in need of such light and love.

And now, cross the threshold that links the ordinary to the fantastical.

You push open the enormous castle doors, surprised at how easily they swing inward. The momentum carries you inside with such force you nearly stumble, but you regain your balance and harness the momentum to quick-march down the hall that leads to the throne.

"You can stop this!" you cry out. You're not even sure who reigns over this land, but you're confident it doesn't matter. You've brought the words to whomever needs to hear them. "People are dying. You must act now!" You're quite happy with yourself. You've undoubtedly completed your mission. "I can help you," you add.

But the Great Hall is vacant and the throne is empty. Your voice careens off one wall and then the next. You slowly draw to a halt. "Is anyone here?" you ask, and the echo of your own voice mocks you.

A robed figure steps out from behind the throne. He has a graying beard and a gnarled old staff not unlike your own. "You're quite right about many things and quite wrong about several others," the wizard chuckles. "But it is good to see you all the same."

You point an uncertain finger. "You . . ."

"It is, just so! But now, to your pressing concerns. People are dying and someone must act and why can't it be you?"

"I don't have the—I thought the ruler of this land would—"

The wizard nods, somber. "This land," he says. A grin plays along the wrinkles of his cheeks. He gestures slightly and the long and heavy curtains that had lined the keep roll upward, revealing the lands beyond the castle walls.

Lands that are curiously peaceful and absent of any bloodshed. Lands that barely resemble the plain you just rode across. Even the city itself has vanished. You're someplace new.

"I—there was a war," you stammer.

"There is a war," the wizard agrees. "Everywhere. And peace is indeed what we seek. But there is no one here to find it but you. And even so, I wonder if you've not already found exactly that, or at least what you yourself require." He gestures at your chest with his staff. "Perhaps it's not the finding we need but the sharing." He smiles.

And you sit heavily in a cushioned red chair that most certainly was not behind you even a moment before.

We are tempted to run to the castle on the hill. But have we forgotten the power that lies within our own inner temple?

THE THIRTY-SECOND CONTEMPLATION

The Talisman, or, That Which We Imbue with Value

Step into adventure.

The wizard pulls up a chair and sits down across from you. He leans back, pulling at his beard, pensive. At some point, you know not when, the torches adorning the walls of the Great Hall had been lit and now the flames are dancing throughout the darkening chamber. You feel as though there are rather large holes in your story. Yet, since you've long accepted that magic is at work here, some force beyond your understanding, you simply lean back and enjoy the warmth those flames cast and the comfort that ensues.

"A great adventure, then," the wizard muses. "I hope, at least."

"Great?" you ask.

"Both enjoyable and consequential," the wizard replies as though you'd asked for a definition of terms. He leans forward, his eyes twinkling. "And I see you've collected some souvenirs along the way."

"Some what?"

"Never as quick as we'd like," a new voice interjects. "But learning all the same." Your spirit guide materializes next to the wizard. The being is hard to see, glimmering in and out of this plane of existence. But you think you detect a grin of sorts on its animal-like snout.

"We all learn in our own time," the wizard says. "In the unfolding of time," the wizard adds with a laugh. "We shake out the great bedsheet of time and who can say what might fall from its crumpled corners?" The wizard gestures at your walking stick.

"What, this?" you say. "My staff? But you gave that to me."

"Did I?"

"And—" you ferret around in your pocket, producing the stones. "These, I suppose. You planted them, too, right?"

The wizard makes a harrumphing sound. "A stick and some old rocks? I can't hardly imagine."

"What?" you ask. "They're magic! And the staff has the runes . . ." Your voice trails off. This must be a test. One more, for good measure.

"Fruit of the earth," the wizard says simply. "But it was the work of your hands that brought the magic."

"I don't have any magic," you say.

"Perhaps you're right," the wizard says, though not to you. The wizard is looking at where the spirit guide had been standing only a moment earlier. "Not as quick as we'd like. But time continues to unfold, and I for one can wait."

Another smile.

Turn to the ordinary.

My grandmother had a great devotion to the Infant Jesus of Prague. At least, I think she did. Seems that most Italian Catholic grandmothers do. Mine had a dozen or so statues in a variety of shapes and sizes depicting the baby Jesus all decked out in royal red, with a crown on his head and a blue orb-with-cross (the *globus cruciger*) in his hand. At the very least, I think it's a safe bet to say she thought highly of this unusual royal baby.

The story behind the Infant Jesus of Prague is curious and convoluted. It has much to do with Carmelites and perhaps even St. Teresa of Ávila herself. As with many saints and holy objects, there's a bit of legend, a bit of lore, and a hint of the miraculous in the story, but none of that matters to me. Or, better stated, the Infant Jesus of Prague statuette is displayed in my bedroom not because of the mysterious voice that emanated from the original image, which was unearthed from the debris of a war-torn church in 1637.

I display it because it once belonged to my grandmother.

This particular holy item has taken on a meaning beyond the obvious. When I look at it, I don't only see Jesus; I see my grandmother. My mind goes to her and to her prayer life, to how this common statuette affected her faith journey. The Infant Jesus of Prague—whether I see it on the shelf in my bedroom or in a church sanctuary—immediately summons my grandmother, making her more than a mere memory. She stands there in the room with me, and together we are enveloped in mystery. Together we continue to go to God.

All to say, these little items that we pick up along the way, these trinkets and prayer cards and holy stones, become important not only because they themselves pierce the veil of the transcendent glistening all around us. They assume deeper meanings because they carry on the spiritual legacy of someone else. We hold a talisman in our hands that pierced the veil for someone we love, and now we hope it might do something similar (though different) for us. These aren't simply heirlooms. These are precious relics, keys to the Other Side, that have served previous believers and now fall to us to use for the greater good—our own and that of others. And as we do, as we place these proverbial keys into the transcendent gates, we pour out new meaning, new significance, new holy energy into these once-simple items. Perhaps others will take them up when we're gone, adding to their storied legacy.

And now, cross the threshold that links the ordinary to the fantastical.

The stones feel cool in your hand, no matter how hard you stare at their varied colors. You try to will the magic to work, to break forth and pour all over the room. But nothing happens. And so you close your fist.

"It's already here," the wizard says, looking at the stones in your hand. "What you seek. Those—" and here, he gestures at your closed fist—"are not for moments such as this. But hold fast to the memory of when they were needed, for the memory will make real the magic in the moment most pressing."

You shake your head, frowning. "Sure," you say. You place the stones back in your pocket, lay your staff across your lap. "So it was all for this: to collect a few trinkets to bring back home?"

The wizard stands, quite suddenly, his blue robes swirling with the movement. "You bring back more than trinkets," he says, a touch of irritation in his voice. "You bring back all of this." He gestures to you—all of you. "But even the sharpest of memory fades and when it does, then, I hope, you reach for those so-called trinkets. They will lead you back."

"Here?"

"Not here," he scowls. "But to where we all arrive now and then. To where we all need a bit of help returning to." A sad smile, then, as the wizard gazes out at the setting sun. "There are heights to which we all climb, and many of us reach them. But we cannot remain at those high altitudes. We quite literally have our breath taken away. We can remember the view, though. I wonder: Will you help others remember, even when you cannot?"

"With stones, a sword, and a stick?"

"With the magic you've already found and placed within them. The magic I'm sending you back to share. It's the magic that continues to work in a stubborn and brave fool like yourself, in spite of it all." And again, the wizard laughs.

The talismans we possess anchor us to moments of profundity. Who do we see when we remember? And why?

THE THIRTY-THIRD CONTEMPLATION

The Phoenix, or, The Spiritual Burn

Step into adventure.

"I have one final trinket for you," the wizard says. He's pacing the width of the Great Hall, his staff tapping gently upon the old stone floor. You sit watching, waiting. What more can be expected of you? What more can you do with the wizard's strange gifts?

But then he turns. He tugs forth something from within the folds of his blue robe. It's small and red and glowing. You stand. You step closer. You feel a strange warmth radiating from this odd—

"It's an egg?" you ask.

"Just so," the wizard says. He hands it to you. Warmth spreads into your fingertips and up your arms. You're careful to hold the little thing with both hands. You realize it's awash in swirling patterns that remind you of the movements and color of smoke. It feels both more solid and more fragile than you'd expected.

The wizard, meanwhile, is chanting something. He holds the base of his staff, pointing the length of the gnarled wood at the far wall. He's twirling it, singing now. And then—

He pulls fire from the torches to his staff as though he's caught a trout on his fishing line. He reels in the dancing flames, summoning them to his feet in a raging, beautiful, circular blaze.

He extends the palm of one hand. Reluctantly, you return the egg to his care.

"This egg," he says, "is uncommon." He holds it close to his crooked nose, nods once, and then casts the fragile thing into the flames.

You gasp.

"But a phoenix egg," the wizard continues, ignoring your panic and dismay, "is meant to be different. To break the mold, as it were." You notice the flames begin to dance higher. You realize you didn't hear the sound of shattering shells, the noise you'd expected. Instead, you detect an unusual slurping noise.

"And why?" the wizard continues. "The phoenix is a cycle. It sustains itself. Or it can, if we allow nature to take its course."

TURN TO THE ORDINARY.

The phoenix has a neat party trick.

Depending on the mythological tradition in question, this firebird of lore is reborn from its own ashes. Imagine: You meet a fiery end and everything literally goes up in flames. And then—*poof*! From the debris and rubble of life, you return. Renewed. Restored. Reborn.

A *really* neat party trick, especially if your party takes an unfortunate turn.

In the phoenix myth, we find a helpful parallel to spiritual seasons focused on death and rebirth, conversion and renewal. In the Christian tradition, we might think of Lent. The phoenix is a literal story of resurrection: what seemingly ends in ash and death is transformed into new life. The phoenix is often associated with the sun and with purifying flames. The spiritual similarities basically write themselves.

But while we may see the overarching parallels between a season like Lent and the legend of the phoenix, what's really important for our own spiritual journeys is this question: Where in the phoenix cycle are we?

Lent begins on Ash Wednesday. Figuratively speaking, we stand in the ashes of last year's palms, which we smear across our foreheads. We imagine ourselves as the phoenix. What was once new and vibrant is now gone and decayed. Is this our moment of incineration? Are the forty days that follow meant to be our own gradual rebirth? Like a spiritual movement that culminates on Easter? Or are those smudged ashes on our foreheads simply the forerunners of the full-bodied pile of ash we necessarily become? Said differently, are we still burning? Are we still on fire? Are those late hours of Holy Saturday like our own personal phoenix moment, the eruption of new life within us from whatever we roasted during the previous forty days?

You might be saying, "Eric—who cares? It's all semantics. We rise on Easter all the same."

And I say, "Yes, but. Have you ever seen a phoenix reborn from a phoenix only half-burned? Can you rise from ashes when you are not yet ashes?"

And you say, "Shut up, Eric. You're making an awful big fuss over a fake bird."

Here's the thing: I think it's important to know where we are in our phoenix cycle. And I think the answer can—and probably should—be different for all of us. But the process of *rebirth from ashes* is necessarily different from the process of *burning away.* We ask different questions. We have different tasks yet to complete.

If we are already being reborn during Lent or some other season in our lives, then we should use this final sprint to our own resurrection moment to ask questions like these:

- What will this new life look like for me?
- How am I invited to delve deeper into who God has remade me to be?
- What role must the Risen Lord play in my life?

But if we are still burning, then we wrestle with different types of questions:

- What of my old ways do I still cling to, and how can I let go?
- What unhelpful things—habits, objects, relationships—have hold over me?
- Is something in me resistant to God's purifying love?

Where are you in *your* phoenix cycle? Was your own moment of ash and dust a transition from one state to another, or was it the beginning of the end of the current state?

"Semantics," you say. "We all burn in the end."

But do we? Or—if we're not careful, not intentional, not aware of our own moment—might we get stuck somewhere in the middle? Might we become some half-burned feathered monster, unable to either let go or look ahead?

I wonder if the worst-case scenario is becoming trapped in a status quo that is both up in flames and untenable, and yet clinging to it all the same.

And now, cross the threshold that links the ordinary to the fantastical.

You stare into the fire, trying to suppress your worry. The wizard has proven to be trustworthy so far, but still. You're not sure throwing a small egg into a pile of flames was the best idea. Certainly not a rational one.

"I thought you were giving that to me," you say. "I thought it was mine."

"It is," the wizard replies. "But look closely and tell me what you see."

"Fire and smoke," you reply. "I'm not sure I can bring that back with me."

"The phoenix sustains itself," the wizard says in return. "Death and resurrection. Ash and rebirth. But what is it you see? Do you see a creature burning, or one being born?"

You stare at the flames, trying to decipher the shapes and sounds and twirling, swirling smoke. Something is moving in that blaze. Is it a dying baby bird, or a baby bird arriving at new life?

"How hard it is," the wizard says, "to see rebirth when we clothe ourselves in the trappings of death. But keep watching. The cycle must continue. Nature will follow its course. And you, my friend, will have a baby phoenix to show your friends back home—that is, when it's old enough to find its way to you." A chuckle.

"Home," you whisper.

"Indeed," the wizard says, placing a hand on your shoulder. "The cycle continues. The patterns. The rhythm of all things."

The phoenix burns and returns
and burns once more.
Where in the phoenix cycle are we?

THE THIRTY-FOURTH CONTEMPLATION

The Return, or, The Inevitable Ending

Step into adventure.

You gaze out upon the road before you—long, winding, and quiet. You inhale deeply, close your eyes. You've come to the end. And now it's time to go home.

You wonder if it was worth it.

"We're tempted to see the road back as a simple retracing of steps," the wizard says, coming alongside you. He seems older. Smaller. He leans heavily on his own gnarled staff. "But it's a new adventure altogether."

"I don't know that I want another adventure," you say. "Just retracing my steps feels like too much right now. I don't know that I've got it in me."

The wizard turns to you. His gaze falls upon your face. You feel a warmth and a consolation in your heart. "But you've not gone this way before," he says.

You furrow your brow, turning to him. "Then you better give me a map."

A smile. "What I mean is, the YOU you are now is different from the YOU you were then. The YOU you are now has not been this way before. Except, of course, you have. You may be retracing steps, but it's with feet that are more attuned to the curves of the road."

"More blistered, you mean. And sore."

The wizard gently taps his staff on the dirt road before him. He looks back over his shoulder, as though he has someplace else to be. But he remains with you all the same, here, in this quiet glen of shade and peace. "I wonder what new things you'll see as you go," he says. "Or, I wonder how you'll see old things anew. And I wonder why you'll see them now and not before, or perhaps even after."

"I wonder if I'll reach home again at all," you say in response. There's a cloud overhead and you're not sure whether it's brought rain or relief from the sun.

Turn to the ordinary.

Mythologist Joseph Campbell is quite clear that a hero's journey requires a return. The story is not finished until a hero goes home and bestows some new learning, wisdom, or benefit upon their place of origin. What seems like the end of the story is actually a new beginning, when "the hero shall now begin the labor of bringing the runes of wisdom" back to their community.[63] The journey was never solely for the hero's benefit. The transformation of self that has occurred can and should serve the common good. We've learned so much! Now it's time to share that learning with others.

Yet, in this moment of return, temptation abounds. Campbell cautions against inventing "a false . . . image of oneself as an exceptional phenomenon in the world."[64] He knows how easy it is for a would-be hero to return from a quest filled with self-righteousness and bloated pride. The goal of the journey, Campbell insists, is a reconciliation between self and "the universal will"—here, we might say, the will of God and the good of all people. God is necessarily concerned with the flourishing of all creation. That means

God's Spirit is constantly breathing new life into all things. The hero must reconcile what they've learned about themselves with what the world needs; the hero must bridge the journey that was with the journey that is yet unfolding, the singular quest with the communal potential. Campbell writes, "The hero is the champion of things becoming, not of things become."[65] *Becoming* insists on ongoing change, ongoing growth, ongoing development. If we wallow in a false sense of superiority, we ultimately become what we sought to destroy: a broken status quo.

I'm struck by Campbell's caution: As we make our necessary return, we do so with the good of others in mind. We know we've gone through an important change; we've grown in ways yet to be fully understood. But this does not mean we rest on our laurels, nor does it mean we are superior to others. Rather, we embrace the fact that the story goes on. We contribute to something still unfolding.

In the end, we must make that return. I believe in doing so, we come face-to-face with whatever has been learned or gained. Even if it's unclear now, in making that return, we acquire that needed clarity; we discover what God has called forth within us for the good of the world. What new insight into ourselves must we share with others? What new wisdom into creation's mysteries can we offer?

Is this too abstract or too grand? Think instead of those times you return from a vacation or a trip. Don't you have souvenirs to give to your friends and family? Stories to tell? Landmarks that you wish to encourage others to see?

I once went to Ireland to lead a series of retreats. It was a deeply consoling trip, satisfying on both personal and professional levels. I had found an inner peace that so often eludes me in my day-to-day. When it came time to return home, though I had my bags packed with souvenirs for my family, my real prayer was to bring that same peace back with me and share it. In fact, my greatest desire was to *be* that peace in my family. Too often I snap at my kids, or grow irritated with the many tasks at hand. What I wanted, having gone on my own little Irish quest, was to bring back this new way of being, this discovery into myself, and live it out for the good of my immediate community. A simple yet poignant prayer for any return journey.

There are other temptations to face when we make our return. On the one hand, we may wonder if we really accomplished anything. On the other hand, we may find ourselves desolate, sad, or dejected because we don't want the adventure to end. We worry that our value at home among our friends will pale in comparison to who we were and what we accomplished on the road.

Both concerns stem from the same lie: Our value is not intrinsic but something we prove either by bringing back something great or by being great on an adventure.

Having made the journey through this book, we may return with good things—I hope we do!—and we may have proven something about ourselves along the way. But I hope that our journey through these many pages has revealed that the Holy Spirit is already at work in us. We don't need to prove anything; we simply need to pay attention. By living as our authentic selves, by allowing God to work uniquely through our lives and vocations, we are all we need to be. And then, still, God continues to draw out something new from our lives, calling something beautiful out of each of us.

The so-called boons of our journey arrive organically because we've committed to being who we already are. They grow out of the well-fertilized soil of our souls, blossoming into abundance. By making that return, we allow God to work in us for the good of others, in our own communities.

Jesus makes a return. It's called the Resurrection. It's a quiet affair. He goes to see his friends; he shares meals with them and offers them his reflections. He gives them encouragement and then sends them forth. He walks with them *even when they're going the wrong direction*, as was clear in Jesus's encounter with the disciples on the road to Emmaus.

Jesus brings with him the boon of new life, a new way of living, a new level of possibility to fuel dreams and hopes (i.e., the resurrection of the dead!). He's the same, but different, changed by and for this next leg of the journey. Significantly, he patiently accompanies his friends, his community. He does not extol his virtues, even though he certainly could have. Instead, he continues along his Way.

So too are we changed. So too are we still on the road. As you reflect back on your own journey through these pages and through this season of your life, you can only discover that you are YOU . . . and yet, you are also something new. Give thanks for that transformation and then go out into the world to share it.

And now, cross the threshold that links the ordinary to the fantastical.

And so you've come to it at last.

"You're not coming with me?" you ask, realizing the truth.

"No," the wizard says. "There are other places and other people that require my attention. But you have what you need. You are who you need. And remember this—" the wizard taps you on the shoulder with his staff— "that which you see anew is speaking anew to you. So pay attention to what catches your attention. Those are the tiny glimmers of light shining a spotlight upon your soul."

You smile and shake your head. "Thanks, I guess," you say, extending a hand.

The wizards takes it. He nods. "Gratitude is both balm and sustenance. I imagine you'll be chewing on those specific things you guess you're thankful for as you go along the way."

You open your mouth to say something witty in reply. But before you're able to summon even a single word, the wizard vanishes and you're left alone once more.

The return is an intrinsic part of the journey.
What do we bring back with us?
Who are we becoming for the good of others?

THE THIRTY-FIFTH CONTEMPLATION

The Mage, or, The Role You Play in the Sequel

STEP INTO ADVENTURE.

The tea is too hot to sip, but you hold the mug carefully cradled in two hands all the same, enjoying the warmth against your skin. You sit at your small kitchen table, looking out the window at the rolling hills leading away from your home. The vast blue sky is dotted with an occasional cloud. It's a peaceful existence. Quiet. A bit secluded, perhaps, but you're not without visitors.

In fact, you're studying such visitors now: a gaggle of three young folks picking their way up the path. They look eager and afraid, and they move with an urgency that betrays their intentions.

They've come to see you. More to the point, they need something.

You set down your tea and push yourself away from the table. You wonder what this band of travelers is after, what adventure they've set themselves upon. You smile, recalling your own adventures. You grab your staff—leaning on it a bit more heavily than in the past—and scoop up the magic stones from a bowl on your counter and head down the hall.

You open the door just as the three travelers stumble up on your front porch. Your timing always impresses strangers. Gives the illusion of magic. Puts them at ease—like they know they've come to the right place—while also granting yourself just a touch of otherworldliness.

"Hello, there," you say with a grin.

"We've come a long way to find you," the first says, a young woman with hair tied up in a high ponytail. She has an old sword strapped to her back and the look of someone who hasn't yet had reason to use it. Her voice is frantic. "We need your help."

"What you need," you say, "is to come in and rest. You look tired."

"There's no time," another of the group says, a young man with a shock of red hair and a freckled face. "We can't rest."

"But you can have tea," you say, already turning away from the strangers. "It's hot and waiting."

"You were—expecting us?"

"Was I?" you say, with a twinkle in your eye. "In any case, cold tea is no way to begin an adventure."

TURN TO THE ORDINARY.

I wonder about the roles we cast for ourselves in life's many stories. How often and how desirable it is to imagine ourselves as the hero, the one leading the charge, on the frontlines of change, or protest, or the fight for something new. It's a tantalizing image. Indeed, as you've prayed through these pages, perhaps you've seen in yourself this hero, the one who boldly goes into new lands, standing up against treacherous foes. There's a thread of that narrative in all our stories.

But there is another kind of hero. I was interviewing Dean DeBlois, the writer and director responsible for the *How to Train Your Dragon* franchise, about the live-action adaptation. DeBlois was reflecting on one of the story's protagonists, Hiccup, the lackluster dragon slayer and son of the Viking chief.

If you know the story, then you know that Hiccup is a terrible warrior. He's clumsy and always in the way. When he finally has his chance to kill a dragon, his own inner compass refuses to allow him to deliver the fatal blow. Having failed to kill the dragon, Hiccup instead spends time with the creature. As the days pass, Hiccup learns through experience what his teachers never taught him: The terrifying myths of his people are simply untrue. Dragons are not evil creatures but rather possible friends and allies. This was a truth glimpsed only through encounter and relationship, curiosity and love. This, of course, is the greatest of sins for a culture built on slaying dragons! But this is exactly why Hiccup is the hero this story needs. His own experience demands that he reassess the old stories, the status quo. Perhaps dragons aren't the villains the Vikings believed them to be.

As DeBlois explained, Hiccup is a *teaching* hero, not because he's a great warrior but precisely because he's not. "He has the courage and the capacity, the empathy to look beyond that age-old teaching and to find that, oh, there's more to this story, more to this perceived enemy," DeBlois said. "Just by having the courage to march to the beat of his own drum and to defy tradition, he finds a way forward that actually uncovers the baseless fear [in his community] and finds the real root of the problems so that coexistence [becomes] possible."

A *teaching* hero, it seems to me, is also a *prophetic* hero, one who points toward a new way of living and relating that may seem all but impossible given a current broken status quo. But this teaching hero dares to dream, dares to imagine and, most importantly, dares to be comfortable in their own skin. Such a hero points to a hoped-for future even as they name the thing that keeps the community tethered to an undesirable present.[66]

As we conclude this shared adventure, we recognize that the story goes on. But our role in the continuing journey must necessarily change. We are not always the protagonists. We may suddenly realize that we've become the mentor figure in someone else's story. (After all, we can't be the hero in someone else's story! We can only be a guide, lest we become a villain intent on bending another to our will.) We have been to the other side, seen what's possible, glimpsed something of God's dream. We've brought it back, too, and shared it with our community. And still the story goes on. Now, we're called to offer what we know, what we've learned, to the next generation. We humbly step back, when appropriate, to allow others to step forward. But because we care about this community, about society, about the People of God, we always offer generously whatever we can.

I think about Plato's Allegory of the Cave. As we perceive and experience God's own grace breaking into our stories, do we not have a responsibility to go back and share it with others? I believe any true experience of God necessarily leads to our sharing that experience. God's own self overflows within us, a holy abundance. The Christ within us calls us to the Christ within others.

Jesus is a teaching hero. His whole ministry was about showing the way to a new understanding of life, of relationships, of purpose and meaning. He sent his followers out on mission. That's the whole Christian project: to accompany others into this new way of life. To remind people that God is a God of grace who appears quite suddenly, inviting us to turn and see the ordinary with new eyes.

God does not desire that we remain in anybody's cave; in fact, this is why Jesus arrived on the scene. This is why Christ pursues the lost sheep: to help us see we are made for something more!

We are made in the image and likeness of this same God. It is our responsibility, then, to point the way to this God of surprises. It is our responsibility to walk with others into this new way of living, to shatter those broken status quos. It is our responsibility to become the teaching hero.

And now, cross the threshold that links the ordinary to the fantastical.

You can tell that your guests are not enjoying their tea. They are restless, eyes darting around your small kitchen, feet tapping against the floor.

You sit at the head of the table. "Well, then," you say. "The tea is getting cold, and I suspect you won't find many warmer cups than these where you're all headed."

"How do you know where we're headed?" the woman asks, suspicious.

"I don't," you say with a shrug. "Nor do I know from where you've come. But I'll hazard a guess that neither of those answers are half as important as why you're going in the first place."

"We have to save our village," the third of your guests interjects. "We heard you had magic. That you could help."

You nod, thoughtful. "But why?" you ask finally.

The three travelers exchange exasperated looks. "Why?"

"Why," you say. "Or, for what? What new thing is stirring in you? And how might it change your village?"

"We don't want to change the village," the woman says. "We need to save it. We're looking for magic, not—" she waves her hand as though to take in all of you.

You nod again, standing. "You'll find the magic you need when you find the answers to those questions. But in the meantime,"—you reach into your pocket and offer an outstretched hand—"take these. Perhaps they'll help. Maybe they'll show you the way to that new thing you seek."

Your three guests look with wonder at the magic stones resting in your palm. The woman cautiously reaches out, takes one. And you smile.

We become the mage simply by paying close attention to our own journeys—and others now come to us seeking wisdom.
What do we need to do to accept this new role?

Visit me at ericclaytonwrites.com for additional imaginative scenes and resources as you continue your contemplative journey.

PART III

Tools for Sharing

APPENDIX I
Questions for Reflection

Use these questions for your own personal prayer, in small group gatherings, or when facilitating a retreat.

- In what ways do you see your life as an adventure? In what ways do you wish to inject a more adventurous spirit into your daily life?
- What contemplation most resonates with where you are now in your life? Why?
- What contemplation caused you to pause or left you feeling desolate? Why?
- Return to the Pray-er Worksheet you completed at the outset of this book's journey. Compare with the new answers you can write on pages 263–265. How have you grown and developed? Where might you head next?
- Are there mythic or fantastical tropes or motifs that did not appear in these pages that you find useful in your own spiritual journey? What are they, and why are they helpful for you?
- As you prayed through a particular contemplation, did the faces of people from your daily life come to mind? How might these individuals be playing the roles of fantastical characters (that is, the guide, the bard, the companions, and others)? How might you bring your

real-life relationships into dialogue with these mythic motifs? How might these mythic motifs illuminate the roles of your real-life relationships?

- It can be hard (or even feel silly) to look at the world as fantastical, as a place where the spiritual and temporal so readily meet. In what ways have you identified resistance within yourself to seeing the world as grace-filled and pulsing with the supernatural?
- As you reflect on your personal history with myth, fairy tales, and fantasy, call to mind some of your earliest memories of these genres. What stories shaped you? Do the contemplations in this book pull on any of those early memories? How?
- What contemplation surprised you? Were you challenged to reimagine or reframe your approach to a fantastical motif? Did the reframing change how you see something in yourself?
- Return to any contemplation. Reread the "Step into adventure" section. Then, stop. What story from your own life does this rereading evoke in you? What memories are stirred?
- Do you feel a particular call or invitation to step into the unknown right now in this moment in your life? Where is it coming from? What does it ask of you?
- What is your current status quo? How might a step into the unknown help you disrupt it?
- How does your understanding of and reflection on the world of Fairie help you better understand and enter more deeply into relationship with God? How do fairy tales help you better grapple with God's dream for our world?

- How does the structure of myth and legend help you better grasp and enter into the story of Jesus? Do you see Jesus as a mythic hero? How does this framing deepen your understanding of our God who speaks through story?
- Why do you believe God speaks to us through stories? Why might God use mythic structures in communicating Truth to help us better grasp reality?
- What strengths and gifts does this fantastical journey reveal in you? What challenges and shadows does it reveal?
- What are you being asked to bring back to your community at journey's end? To what community do you return?
- How do you feel when the story ends? What emotions does it stir in you?
- How do you feel about your shifting role in the story? Are you able to move from hero to mentor? Who are you being invited to accompany? How can you do so? How can you walk with another in their own epic adventure?

APPENDIX II

Formatting a Retreat or Workshop

The contemplations of this book are organized to reflect the general three-act storytelling structure of the "Hero's Journey." (I owe a lot to Jessica Brody's *Save the Cat! Writes a Novel* for my own understanding of how this sort of story can be structured. Her framing influences what follows.) These three acts, broadly speaking, invite a protagonist to (1) respond to a catalyst that interrupts their ordinary lives by answering a call that (2) propels them into an upside-down world in which they are confronted by challenges and encouraged to grow so that (3) they return to their communities transformed and able to revolutionize the status quo they left behind.

Transformation of the protagonist is key to any good story. So, too, is transformation our hope in a retreat context. How might our hearts be transformed so as to be more ready and able to love and serve God and neighbor?

This storytelling structure is reflected in *The Spiritual Exercises of St. Ignatius*, a retreat meant to help individuals discover who they really are so that they can better align themselves to God's dream for their lives. Transformation is necessarily at play.

A retreatant prays through four spiritual movements or "weeks" that we can roughly map onto this storytelling structure. Mapping four weeks onto three acts may sound ham-handed, so let's leave the three acts to the side and instead focus on how particular plot beats are mirrored in the four weeks of the Exercises.

In the First Week, retreatants assess their broken status quo, looking closely at their own personal shortcomings and those present in the wider world. The way most stories begin for a heroic protagonist (Look at how things are! Oh, how I wish they were different!) is analogous to us in our relationship with God. God does not wish for retreatants to stay in a broken way of life or to wallow in sin and guilt. God calls retreatants out and into the world, to walk with Jesus. Again, this bears an uncanny resemblance to how protagonists are called to adventure: They leave behind their old lives to step into the unknown.

In the Second Week, retreatants reflect on Jesus's ministry of healing and accompaniment, journeying with him in their imaginative engagement with Scripture. Jesus's ways are not our ways; seeing how he lives is truly an encounter with an upside-down world where the last are first and the blind can see. Jesus, too, is our mentor as he guides us into this new way of life. We are asked to allow ourselves to be transformed by encounters with Christ as well as by people living on the margins. Seeing how Jesus treats people society views as outsiders reveals to us a radically different way of living. In fact, in preaching on the Kingdom of God, Jesus is inviting us to imagine a completely other world, one that runs counter to the world as we know it!

But then, in the Third Week, we enter a dark night, witnessing the Passion and death of our friend and mentor. (Any good story has one final test for a protagonist, the moment where all seems lost and a hero either persists or gives up.)

This darkness is dispelled in the Fourth Week: Jesus rises from the dead, returns to his friends and, importantly, sends his disciples (i.e. the retreatants!) out into the world. As were the disciples, retreatants, entrusted now with a new role in manifesting God's dream for creation, are transformed. The work of living the

Gospel begins in our homes, our places of business, our schools, our local communities. (Think of the stories you love. How many of them require the protagonist to return to their old lives informed by the lessons learned on their adventures, but now they are ready and willing to do their part in changing the status quo? This is an essential plot point!)

Informed by both the spiritual insights of the Exercises and the narrative framework of the three-act story structure, we can make use of the contemplations in this book in important ways.

Beginning with the Pray-er Worksheet, retreatants articulate the opening pages of their story. How do they see themselves at the outset? What is their status quo?

From there, we can follow the story beats we've just articulated from the Spiritual Exercises. Retreat leaders can use whichever contemplations are most helpful to retreatants as they grow in self-discovery and relationship with God and others. However, it's suggested that any retreat be designed around these four specific story beats: the call (Contemplation 1); the crossing of the threshold (Contemplation 8); the dark night (Contemplations 29 and 30); and the return (Contemplations 34 and 35).

The contemplations of this book can be broken down as follows:

- Contemplation 1 mirrors the call to adventure, introducing readers and retreatants to the idea of a guide who invites them beyond their status quo.
- Contemplations 2–7 provide an opportunity for readers and retreatants to reflect on their status quo and those many points of inner resistance to stepping into the unknown. Likewise, these contemplations invite reflection on the strengths and opportunities that embracing adventure can provide.

- Contemplation 8 is the necessary crossing-the-threshold contemplation that thrusts readers and retreatants into the upside-down world.
- Contemplations 9–25 comprise what we might consider Act 2 of this book's narrative. This is where the readers and retreatants really explore the upside-down world, meet with conflict and challenge, mine the depths of their own experience, and begin to discover something new about themselves.
- Contemplations 26–31 break into Act 3 and the final confrontation. Contemplations 29–30 make up the dark night of this particular journey where our protagonist is faced with existential choices.
- Contemplations 32–35 comprise the return sequence, pulling together threads from the full scope of the book and inviting the readers and retreatants to synthesize what has been learned as they prepare to offer something to their own community. Specifically, Contemplations 34–35 showcase the return.

In addition to the core contemplations that comprise the call, threshold, dark night, and return, retreat leaders are encouraged to select an appropriate number of additional contemplations for retreatants to reflect upon, as time permits and interest allows.

Consider offering a collection of contemplations that invite retreatants to plunge deeply into a particular theme. For example:

- Discerning Spirits—Fairies, Pixies, Shadow, Djinn
- Expanding the Imagination—Genius Loci, Centaur, Vision, Star
- Finding Meaning in the Ordinary—Staff, Stones, Words of Power, Talisman

- Embracing Our Shadows—Winged Terror, Sword, Minotaur, Cave
- Claiming Our Worthiness—Elves, Feast, Bard, Goddess
- Imagining a More Just World—Witches, Knight, Dragon, Castle

APPENDIX III

Activities for Retreats, Classrooms, and Small Groups

Use and expand upon these activities and ideas in your chosen setting and community.

Turn to your ordinary.

Select a contemplation that spoke to you. Pretend there is no essay in the "Turn to the ordinary" section. Instead, write your own. What story from your life does this contemplation evoke? Share it with a partner.

The missing legends.

Was there a creature of myth or a fantastical motif that was missing from this book? What is it? Why is it important to you? What spiritual theme does it evoke? Write your own second-person meditation.

Pop goes the culture.

Choose a current, popular fantastical story (TV show, novel, movie, comic, or video game). What spiritual themes do you detect in this story? What themes resonate with you in your own life? If you were to interrupt the flow of this story—similar to how each contemplation in this book interrupts a fantastical motif—what personal anecdote would you insert to illuminate the themes?

Stories that shape you.

Consider a novel, movie, scene, or character that you love or that is currently resonant in pop culture. Why do these stories or plot points move you, or move others? Bring them into dialogue with one of the contemplations of this book. For example, maybe there's a mythical dragon—Toothless, Smaug—you really love. What happens when you think about that particular dragon in conversation with the contemplation on The Dragon? What new insights are revealed?

The road goes ever on.

Inspired by the contemplations in this book, map out your own epic journey. Put it down on a piece of paper—get creative! What are the stops? What do you learn at each one? Who do you meet and what do you take away?

The bit of truth in legend.

Pick one of the contemplations that speaks most directly to you. Research that motif. If you choose fairies, for example, briefly look up the history of fairies across history, literature, and folklore. What do you find to be most important? What do this specific history and the individual stories say to you? How do they change or expand your spiritual reflections?

The dungeon master.

Pick one of the contemplations that speaks most to you. Craft an original story that leads into that contemplation and/or picks up where the contemplation leaves off. What story elements do you feel are most needed? Where does your story go?

Words of power.

Share a favorite quote from a film, novel, comic, or some other medium. ("All we have to do is decide what to do with the time that is given to us," Gandalf says, by way of example.) Why is this quote meaningful to you? How do others in your group react to it? What spiritual insights does this quote point to, and how is it helpful in daily life? (Similarly, you can do this exercise with a favorite movie scene.)

An epic soundtrack.

Find a song that illuminates the themes or ideas of one of the contemplations. Why does it resonate? How does adding music deepen your experience of the reflections? How does your chosen song affect others?

APPENDIX IV

For Families

Use the activities that follow to bring enchantment into your family's prayer life.

In the garden.

Make a fairy garden using branches, leaves, moss, and more, plus any little fairy-tale figurines you may have on hand. Talk to your children about the care you are taking in preparing a special place for fairies to visit. How does such care reflect how we are called to prepare our own hearts, our own homes for God? How can we create special places in our lives for God's own Spirit to enter? How do we work in tandem with nature?

A family favorite.

Watch or read a family favorite fairy tale. Look for the moment of *eucatastrophe*—that sudden, joyous, surprising turn. This is the breaking-in of grace in the story, a moment of miraculous change. And yet, it's also likely not the end of the story. Talk to your children about how God works in this way in our real lives; God breaks into our story to give us a boost, to shower us with love, to remind us that God continues to dwell with us even in dark times. Can you name examples from your life? How did you respond?

Compare and contrast.

Find two versions of the same fairy tale—for example, Disney's *The Little Mermaid* and Hans Christian Andersen's version of the tale. Review both with your kids. (Remember: The originals are always darker!) How does this layering over of the same tale from different traditions better help you understand the complexity of the characters, setting, and themes? Now, do the same thing with a Gospel story—for example, read the stories of Jesus's birth from different Gospel authors. How do these different tellings help you better understand Christ's birth? How do differences across tellings expand your understanding of these important stories? What new things do you see from hearing different tellings? How do these distinct narratives point to a common truth?

A picture's worth.

Invite your kids to draw a fantastical scene depicting magical creatures from their imagination. Once they have finished their drawing, ask your kids where they first learned about these fairy-tale creatures. How do they know what they look like? Ask for as many details as your kids can provide. Now, ask your children to describe God, the Holy Spirit, or angels. After all, we rarely "see" God, and yet many people have drawn pictures of God. Where have these images and ideas come from? Do they come from stories in the same way that your kids' fairy-tale creatures come from stories? How do we absorb details from these various texts to help us put words and images to the otherwise unimaginable? How might this conversation form and expand your children's religious imagination?

"Finding Fairy Tales with God"
by
Elianna Clayton (6)

Endnotes

1. Andrew Greeley, *The Catholic Imagination* (University of California Press, 2001), 1.
2. Robert A. Segal, *Jung on Mythology* (Princeton University Press, 1998), 6.
3. Segal, 16.
4. Segal, 17.
5. Segal, 19.
6. Pierre Teilhard de Chardin, *Writings*, ed. Ursula King, Modern Spiritual Masters Series (Orbis Books, 1999), 50–51.
7. John Hendrix, *The Mythmakers: The Remarkable Fellowship of C.S. Lewis & J.R.R. Tolkien* (Harry N. Abrams, 2024), 95–96.
8. C. G. Jung, "Myth and Religion" from *Psychology and Religion* in *Jung on Mythology*, ed. Robert A. Segal (Princeton University Press, 1998), 218.
9. J. R. R. Tolkien, *Tales from the Perilous Realm: A Classic Fantasy Anthology of Poetry, Short Stories, and Fairy Tales* (William Morrow Paperbacks, 2021), 375.
10. Tolkien, *Tales from the Perilous Realm*, 384.
11. C. S. Lewis, *Of Other Worlds: Essays and Stories* (HarperOne, 2017), 58.
12. Martin Shaw, *Liturgies of the Wild: Myths That Make Us* (Sentinel, 2026), 35.
13. Gene Wolfe, *Shadow & Claw* (*The Book of the New Sun* 1), (Tor Trade, 2021), ix.
14. Matthew 11:25.
15. Greeley, *The Catholic Imagination*, 1.
16. Gerard Manley Hopkins, "God's Grandeur," https://poets.org/poem/gods-grandeur.
17. Much of this section appeared as an original essay for IgnatianSpirituality.com: https://www.ignatianspirituality.com/catholic-worldbuilding-and-the-ignatian-imagination/.
18. Robert J. Schreiter, R. Scott Appleby, and Gerard F. Powers, eds. *Peacebuilding: Catholic Theology, Ethics, and Praxis* (Orbis Books, 2010), 221, 223.
19. Walter J. Burghardt, SJ, *An Ignatian Spirituality Reader,* ed. George W. Traub, SJ, vol. 1 (Loyola Press, 2008), 89–98.
20. Anthony de Mello, SJ, *Awareness: Conversations with the Masters*, ed. J. Francis Stroud, SJ (Penguin Random House Christian Publishing, 1992), 121.
21. G. K. Chesterton, *Orthodoxy* (Ignatius Press, 1995), https://www.pagebypagebooks.com/Gilbert_K_Chesterton/Orthodoxy/The_Ethics_of_Elfland_p6.html.
22. Shaw, *Liturgies of the Wild*, 52.
23. Jessica Brody, *Save the Cat! Writes A Novel: The Last Book on Novel Writing You'll Ever Need* (Ten Speed Press, 2018).
24. Wolfe, *Shadow & Claw*, viii.
25. Wolfe, ix.
26. J. R. R. Tolkien, *Unfinished Tales: The Lost Lore of Middle-Earth* (Del Rey, 1988), 407.
27. Galatians 5:14.

28. "Prayer to Your Guardian Angel," United States Conference of Catholic Bishops, accessed February 21, 2026, https://www.usccb.org/prayers/prayer-your-guardian-angel.
29. Matthew 5:48.
30. Mark 1:11.
31. John J. English, SJ, *Spiritual Freedom: From an Experience of the Ignatian Exercises to the Art of Spiritual Guidance*, 2nd ed. (Loyola Press, 1995), 264.
32. English, 264.
33. Greg Boyle, SJ, *Cherished Belonging: The Healing Power of Love in Divided Times* (Avid Reader Press / Simon & Schuster, 2024).
34. Boyle, 101.
35. Boyle, 101.
36. Mark 11:15–19.
37. Thich Nhat Hanh, *Anger: Wisdom for Cooling the Flames* (Riverhead Books, 2002), 72.
38. Nhat Hanh, 76.
39. John 18:37–38.
40. Christopher Pramuk, *All My Eyes See: The Artistic Vocation of Fr. William Hart McNichols* (Orbis, 2004), 5.
41. 1 Corinthians 13:12.
42. 1 Corinthians 13:13.
43. Carl McColman, *The Little Book of Christian Mysticism* (Broadleaf Books, 2021), 240.
44. Philippians 2:7.
45. Ezekiel 37:3.
46. Ezekiel 37:5–7.
47. Ezekiel 37:11.
48. George E. Ganss, SJ, *The Spiritual Exercises of St. Ignatius* (Loyola Press, 1992), SE 186, 79.
49. Genesis 3:5.
50. Job 38:4, 6–7.
51. Guy J. Consolmagno, SJ, *A Jesuit's Guide to the Stars: Exploring Wonder, Beauty, and Science* (Loyola Press, 2025), 164–165.
52. Consolmagno, 165.
53. Carl McColmon, *The Little Book of Christian Mysticism: Essential Wisdom of Saints, Seers, and Sages* (Hampton Roads Publishing, 2018), 123.
54. Joseph Campbell, *The Hero with a Thousand Faces* (New World Library, 2008), 92.
55. Campbell, *Hero*, 97.
56. Luke 1:48.
57. Neil Gaiman, *Coraline* (HarperCollins, 2002), epigraph.
58. Boyle, *Cherished Belonging*, 10.
59. Rose Marie Berger, *Choosing Peace: The Catholic Church Returns to Gospel Nonviolence*, ed. Marie Dennis (Orbis Books, 2018), 171.
60. Berger, 177.
61. J. R. R. Tolkien, *The Fellowship of the Ring*, (Ballantine Books, 1965), 92–93.
62. John 2:19–21.
63. Campbell, *Hero*, 167.
64. Campbell, 205.
65. Campbell, 209.
66. Eric Clayton, "Why We Need Teaching Heroes and Other Lessons from *How to Train Your Dragon*," Jesuit Media Lab, https://jesuitmedialab.org/lessons-how-to-train-your-dragon/, 2025.

Acknowledgments

I remember standing in my kitchen talking about the initial seeds of the idea that became this book. My eldest daughter, Elianna, quickly provided me with a working title—"Finding Fairy Tales with God"—and eagerly drafted a cover (you can see that original art in Appendix III). Both she and my younger daughter, Camira, began rattling off a whole host of topics and themes with which to anchor each chapter and, before I knew it, I had a robust working document. I owe the early enthusiasm for this book to Elianna and Camira, and I'm grateful. Their delight and wonder and love of all things fantastical buoys my, at times, jaded soul.

I also remember walking the grounds of the Bon Secours Retreat Center in Marriottsville, Maryland, with a friend, Ryan Carroll, during a session of that year's Jesuit Media Lab's Ignatian Creators Summit. I don't know if he recalls that conversation, but for me it was deeply consoling. We were asking similar questions: *What would happen if we prayed with this stuff? What if we contemplated God-at-work in fantasy and fairy tales? What if we let it affect our spiritual lives?*

These two key moments—taken together with my lifelong love of speculative storytelling and mythic adventures and the Catholic imagination—propelled this project to the page.

I'm thankful that my agent, Keely Boeving, and my friend and executive editor at Loyola Press, Gary Jansen, understood—or at least, *pretended* to understand—my hopes for this manuscript. Their determination, support, ideas, and wisdom helped make this book a reality.

I'm grateful, too, to the whole team at Loyola Press—particularly my editor, Maura Poston, whose patience, encouragement, and grammatical wizardry has once again helped me bring a somewhat off-the-wall book into existence. I'm grateful to the Jesuit Conference of Canada and the United States, and to my colleagues and collaborators in the Jesuit Media Lab, for refueling my Ignatian-inspired creativity time and again. I'm thankful to the many retreatants who attended retreats I have led in the past few years and—perhaps unknown to them—test-drove some of these reflections. Your reflective input has shaped their final form.

Most of all, I'm grateful to my family who has always encouraged (tolerated?) my love of all things fantastical. My parents, my brother, my grandparents, my teachers—the many people who have read my creative writing, who have humored my love of Star Wars, and who have tolerated winding anecdotes about fictional places and magical creatures.

And finally, I'm ever grateful to my wife, Alli, with whom I have the profound pleasure of building a home of magic and wonder and mystery and delight. A home in which we encourage that playful demeanor in ourselves and in our children, a disposition that insists, *Yes, even here something wondrous is taking place. Even here, even now, our God of Surprises is cooking up something out-of-this world.* May we never lose that desire to turn to the ordinary with an eye prepared to be astonished.

About the Author

Eric Clayton is an award-winning writer, speaker, storyteller, and sought-after retreat leader. He is the author of *Finding Peace Here and Now: How Ignatian Spirituality Leads Us to Healing and Wholeness*; *My Life with the Jedi: The Spirituality of Star Wars* (a book that uses Ignatian spirituality to explore the spiritual underpinnings of a beloved space opera); and *Cannonball Moments: Telling Your Story, Deepening Your Faith*. He is the co-author of two books for children: *Our Mother Too: Mary Embraces the World* and *The Seagull on the Chapel: A Story of Value and Worth*. Eric's spiritual writing has appeared in *America Magazine*, *National Catholic Reporter*, *U.S. Catholic*, and many more. His speculative fiction has been published by Air and Nothingness Press, Small Wonders, and others. Eric is the deputy director of communications at the Jesuit Conference of Canada and the United States, where he is a guest host of *AMDG: A Jesuit Podcast*, and writes an award-winning weekly newsletter, *Now Discern This*. He earned a BA in creative writing and international studies from Fairfield University and an MA in international media from American University. He also has a graduate-level certificate from Creighton University's program in the Ignatian tradition. Eric lives with his family near Baltimore.

Connect with Eric:
ericclaytonwrites.com /
ericclayton.substack.com
Facebook @eclaytopia
Instagram @eclaytopia

Pray-er Worksheet: Reflecting on Character

I am ____,

and my adventure begins on ______________________________.

What is the grace you seek from this adventure? Humility? Understanding of purpose? Strength to make a big decision?

____

____

____

____

What are your strengths?

____

____

____

What opportunities for growth stretch out before you?

Is there a holy or wise person, living or deceased, you turn to for guidance in your life? What actions can you take from their insights?

What spiritual tools do you carry on this journey? Your rosary? Prayer cards? Icons? Miraculous medals?

What was your previous spiritual journey? Was it made during a pilgrimage? A retreat? Reading a book that really spoke to you?

What insights did you acquire on that journey that can be brought along on this adventure?

What words of power might you invoke as you set off? Write your prayer to guide you through your journey.

Notes from the Journey

Notes from the Journey